IMPECCABLE SCENE DESIGN

FOR GAME, ANIMATION AND FILM

Scene Design Course by Weiye Yin

CYPI PRESS

Foreword

Dream-catcher in the Fantasy World

As one of the experienced artists in China's CG field, Weiye Yin was originally engaged in oil painting. Weiye started to learn 3D software as early as 1997, and has published works on websites of internationally renowned CG art institutions since 2000. Having soon established his name in this industry, Weiye started to work as a professional. His works were showcased in famous CG art year books and albums such as "*Elemental*," "*Exposé*," "*Painter*," and "*Exotique*." He received Master Award in "*Exposé 5*." One might well say that his works have captured how CG art has developed since its introduction into China in 1990s. Weiye Yin has participated in a number of world-renowned game projects. Having established a well-developed style in scene design, Weiye is proficient at building up a certain ambience. Years of training in traditional artistic forms helped to elevate his works to a new level — his CG works feature appropriate character design, strong sense of color, and a concrete overall understanding of the picture, all reflecting his outstanding artistic accomplishments.

This book has showcased many pieces of scene design works by Weiye Yin. In addition, the artist has used intelligible language to depict the background information, concept development process and interesting details of each piece. The book not only incorporates concrete examples and thorough explanations of CG techniques, but also the artist's personal experience and sparks of inspiration, enabling the readers to make full use of their imagination for more inspiration. To the beginners, this book is an ideal introduction; to the artists with considerable practice in this area, reading this book can enable face-to-face communication and crashes of varied thoughts. Weiye has cooperated with leewiART, an international CG art promotion institution for years. Through our cooperation, his perseverance in art practice and experimentation has deeply moved us. We hope that Yin will present to us more impressive works in the future.

Zheng Yuan

Joint Founder of leewiART

November, 2010, Beijing

Concept and Expansion

In recent years, concept design industry has experienced unprecedented development. The professionals with rich experience and good at thinking are always treasured in this industry. Their inspirations and concepts are not only valuable for the enterprises which they serve and cooperate with, but also priceless for the development of the entire concept design industry and the expansion of concept art field. Due to their efforts, concept design has evolved into an emerging independent artistic form.

In the context of a flourishing video game industry in China, a number of renowned artists, including Weiye Yin, have played a leading role. They have innovatively integrated the oriental and occidental art and design styles and come up with a new approach. Engaged in this profession for years, Weiye is very proficient at manipulating striking visual elements. Every piece of his works is amazing. These works have been themed upon a rich variety of subjects, including fantasy, sci-fi and other areas. Though these works are also based on digital techniques, they are impressive due to their particular styles, unlike ordinary CG illustrations. Moreover, he is capable of handling varied kinds of scene design, and switching between organic architecture and more structured scene in an easy way.

This book can enlighten young artists troubled with insufficient experience, because they can find a lot of information concerning the author's inspirations and thoughts. The author has made detailed explanations relating to these areas. It is believed that this book will faciliate their artistic development. In addition, the artists with considerable experience in this field will also find this book helpful. They will certainly enjoy Weiye's works which boast of remarkable color and impressive appearance. There is no way they will be disappointed.

Therefore, I believe this book will definitely be an outstanding album as a feast to the eyes.

I hope that Weiye will make better performance in this profession!

Sparth

Sparth (Nicolas Bouvier)

November, 2010

Preface

Widely applied, scene design is fundamentally different from common scene depiction, both in an artistic sense and practical sense. The former involves infusing new design elements into the scene, giving it richer connotations and making it more powerfully expressive. Moreover, artists can create fantasy and wonder that do not exist in the real world. This book will enable a profound understanding of the entire process of scene design, presenting to the readers how these wonderful scene design works have come into being.

At the mention of scene design, one cannot skip over CG creation, which currently prevails. As CG techniques apply well to scene design works, more and more artists who were originally engaged in traditional painting have started to commit themselves to CG art. I am one of them.

Before moving into the domain of CG creation, I was mainly focused on oil painting. My works were not about fantasy, but about realistic subjects. Profoundly influenced by the academic school, I seldom touched upon fantasy or sci-fi themes in oil painting, even though these themes are common in my scene design works. Compared with my contemporary, I am more innovative, and more acceptable of novel things. Or else, I would not engage myself in CG and scene design areas.

I am a person who loves dreaming and painting dreams. No matter sleeping or awake, my mind is always filled with a lot of pictures. These pictures have been anchored to my mind. Whenever unoccupied, I will sketch out these pictures on paper to keep track of my thoughts. I had never thought that my love of dreaming and painting dreams have enabled me to embark on a journey of artistic pursuit and provided me with a lot of inspirational ideas.

Foreign blockbusters started to be introduced into China since 1990s. These blockbusters, especially the sci-fi movies have exposed me to charms of CG art. I saw a sci-fi movie called "Star Wars," in which a lot of CG techniques were employed. Depending on the CG techniques and settings, the director has successfully contructed a breath-taking fantasy world. Though this movie seems to be roughly produced today, but it did amaze me at that time. After seeing the movie, I started to collect data for research to explore the wonders of these technical effects and came to have a considerable knowledge of CG and 3D technology. Unfortunately, due to limited functions and inadequate softwares of PC, there was no way to accomplish the special effects at home. Thus, my experimentation scheme came to an abrupt stop. In 1997, I bought a PC equipped with Intel Pentium MMX, after which my experimentation efforts were revived. At that time, I only had access to a 3D software named 3DS 4 operating in the DOS system, which the prevailing 3DS MAX updated from. Though compared with its counterparts, 3DS 4 is not easy to operate and has fewer functions, it enabled me to get an idea of 3D creation in the real sense and allured me into the domain of CG creation. With software and hardware updates as well as popularization of digital tablets, I have come to create my fantasy world with more ease.

Through ten years of exprimentation and practice, I have obtained a considerable understanding of CG art and scene design: fantasy and real worlds are inter-related and inseparate.

Generally speaking, many objects in the fantasy world are actually based on things in real world. Fantasy world resembles dreams, while dreams are constructed upon reality. The artists are those who keep note of fantasy and dreams, and retain the illusory scenery and objects. The artists are supposed to extract, exhibit and embellish. They have translated blurry concepts into concrete images or pictures, presenting them to the audience. It is the same with scene design works in this book. Scene artists are not only constructors in the art realm, but also designers and recorders of fantasy worlds. Though not all the fantasy sceneries can be translated into reality, and that this process will involve a lot of time and efforts, there is always a possibility that any fantasy can come true as long as it exists. Fantasy world can act as a primary driving force for the real world.

Actually, every one is endowed with artistic creativity. On condition that you are willing to, you can use pens or instruments at hand to illustrate the world that you have been dreaming of at any time, even without professional training. No matter ordinary people or experienced artists, every one is equal in the realm of fantasy arts. Because in this realm, ideas are more valuable than skills; besides, every one possesses a fantasy world of his own which awaits exploration. Adept skills will help the artists to come closer to the desired effects and make the process more smooth. One is certain to grasp the skills through endless attempts and tireless efforts, accumulating experience during practice.

Every artist has his own approach and techniques. In this sense, there is no fixed rule in the domain of artistic creation; my own approach is not standard. In this book, I just want to share my own creation experience, concept development process and techniques. Which approach to use depends on the artists' own situations.

For those who just entered this realm, I hope this book can be instructional and helpful. For those with considerable knowledge of this area or even the artists with profound experience, I hope this book can provide opportunities for communication and exchange.

Weiye Yin
November, 2010, Beijing

CONTENTS

Chapter I Introduction of Scene Design

Chapter II Basic Principles and Procedures for Scene Design

Chapter III Trainings in Scene Design

A. Landscape

Chapter I
Introduction of Scene Design

I. Scene Design Is about Designing a World

Also called "landscape design," scene design is applied in game, animation, movie, advertising and other areas. However, no matter which area it is used in, scene design is intended to tell stories and depict main characters. In simple words, scene design involves constructing a virtual landscape based on certain systems of world view. This landscape can be either sourced from the reality, or totally originates from certain illusions. It can be built upon ancient elements, contemporary elements or even the artists' visions of the future. It can even be illusory universe or fantasy world. However, everything must be grounded on certain subjects relating to certain world views. The "subjects" can be a story, someone, or something. It is not easy to demonstrate the world view through visual elements in a rational and credible way. This is because scene designers have to take a lot of considerations, ranging from the social climate, natural environment and historical context, to the supportive characters, alien creatures, props and setting in certain scenes. All these factors belong to the realm of scene design. Therefore, it might be said that scene design is actually concerned with designing a world.

Note: World view is a philosophical term, referring to a person's foundamental conceptions of the whole world. A person's world view is based on his scientifc and systematic understanding of the nature, life, society and spirits. There is no standard definition of "world view" in the game industry. However, it is generally interpreted as the existence of everything in the virtual world, survival rules and the background in which certain things take place.

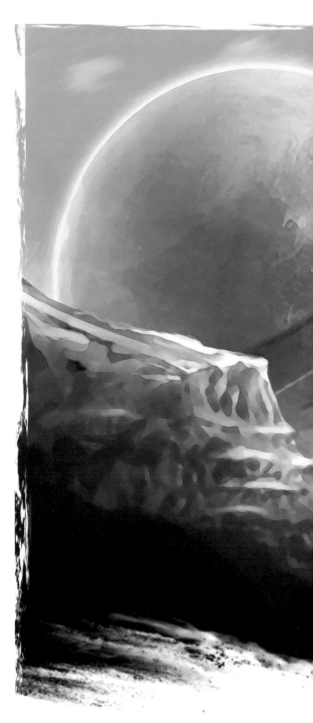

A ratio illustration for multiple-object elements

Take a movie for example. This movie is mainly about a man from the earth who came to another planet, and fell in love with a local girl. Finally, he joined their army to defend the planet against their invaders. The production of this movie requires making a rich variety of landscapes. Besides these landscapes, the artists also have to design all the other elements on this planet, ranging from the landform, climate changes, origin and evolution of species, the social structure and behaviors of all the biomass, to the flowers, birds, fish and insects, as well as rock, sand, dirt and dust. All these designs should be well considered and inter-related. Though some designs seem to be insignificant or rough, in sharp contrast to the rising peaks or winding rivers in the main scenes, they still play an important role considering that credibility will be at stake if the artists have not attached enough attention to these minor elements. What the artists strive to construct is not a presentative scenery, but a coherent virtual entity — an overall structure encompassing the natural environment and social construction. Therefore, every link has to be credible and interdependent. For example, why these rocks can suspend in the air? Why these plants grow like this? Scene design is actually about employing these subtle or uncommon environmental elements

to manifest the artist's world view as well as demonstrate the relationship between different objects and explain the reasons for their existence. Scene design plays an essential role to the overall planning of design conception for the whole project as a remedy to the flaws in the design. An overall scene design scheme as a reflection of the artist's world view also has a significant influence on the design conceptions of main characters and the appearance, features and habits of the creatures. The more complicated the scene designer's world view is, the more considerations he has to take. Of course, the designer can select the "tailoring" function depending on what the design is used for and how complicated his world view is. For example, in some game, animation and movie projects which involve a considerable number of scenarios, the designer can determine on to what extene he will demonstrate his overall world view in this particular project. As for advertising projects, especially those concerned with print advertisements, the designer might have fewer considerations. However, no matter how complicated a world view he intends to demonstrate, the designer has to ensure the integrity and coherence of this world view in every sense.

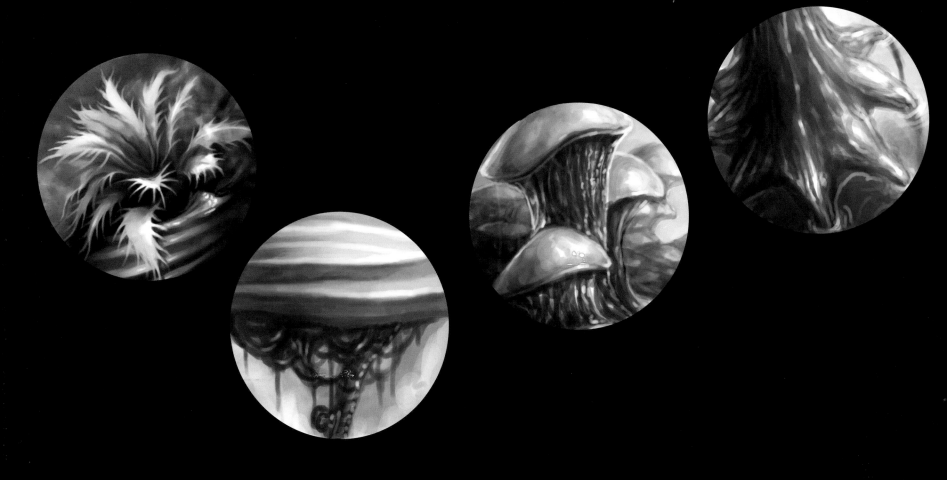

Elevation drawings

II. What Does a Scene Designer Do?

The book is focused on illustrating out how to translate some abstract structural ideas into solid "scene design" schemes, and how to employ some particular expressive approaches in varied categories of scene design projects to realize desired effects. Based on a scene with an integral system of world view, the designer has to visualize all elements such as all the objects, sceneries and ambience in this given scene. This process is defined as "conceptual scene design" by the professionals. "Scene design" schemes are mostly pragmatical, at service of the final effects of commercial projects. Therefore, the integrity of design projects can act as an essential factor to determine whether a particular scene can be eventually wholly produced.

Generally speaking, the designer has to work on the following drawings when doing a particular project: effect drawing, atmosphere drawing, floor plan, elevation drawing, structural drawing (also termed as bird's-eye view), drawing of partial enlargement, as well as explanatory drawing and detail sketch of special sceneries and props involved. A project cannot go smoothly unless all these drawings are integral, precise and coherent.

Elevation drawing of the scene

Structural drawing (bird's-eye view)

In addition, as the perspective in the final movie or animation is already determined, the designer only has to focus on the objects that the camera will cover. However, as to game projects, especially the scenes in which the player can change the perspective at will, the designer has to consider more factors. Besides capturing the characteristics of the scenery from all the perspectives, the designer is also supposed to have a control over how complicated the scenery is and how splendid the finish is, based on certain restrictions such as the performance of the distribution platform for the game and what kind of engine is used. In a word, the designer has to fully exploit the resources available to realize the most ideal effects.

Drawing of partial enlargement

Explanatory drawings for special scenes and props

Atmosphere drawing

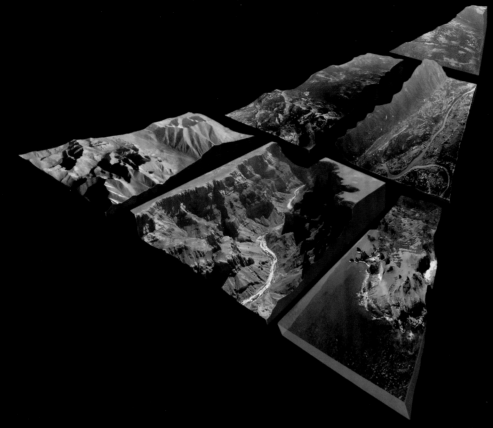

Landform drawing

drawing, the designer is supposed to have impressive capabilities in comprehension and creation. It takes inspirations as well as thinking to accomplish a piece of artwork.

c. A Profound Knowledge of Various Subjects

A designer should depend on a profound knowledge, outstanding vision, and rich life experience to ensure that his works are convincing and credible. Take landscape design for example, which is most commonly used in scene design: landform design is indispensable for any landscape. Such designs must be based on scientific knowledge, because every landscape came into being due to certain factors such as tectonic changes. The designer has to take a lot of considerations, such as the transition from sea to land, the winding of the canyon, the structure of sand dune, the relationship between mountains and rivers, as well as the rising and fall of forested land, and the boundary between plains and wetlands, which means that the designer is supposed to have a considerable knowledge of geography. What is noteworthy is that no matter how tiny-scale a landscape illustration is, the designer would risk making ridiculous mistakes if ignorant of certain geographic phenomena. The more subjects the works concern, the more knowledge the designer needs to grasp.

Besides geography, cultural, religious, historical and racial knowledge should be used to the designer's advantage to produce better works. The more informed and knowledgeable the designer is, the more vivid and meaningful his works will turn out to be. Integral and convincing works will be more likely to impress the viewers and obtain their recognition.

d. A Serious Attitude

The designer has to treat every process seriously, including concept development, selection of subjects, designing, sketching and drawing. His attitudes will affect the quality of the finish.

All these factors will have a direct influence on the effects and meanings of the landscape works, which also determines whether the design works can present particular artistic styles.

III. What Is Required of a Scene Designer?

An excellent scene design project involves consideration of various factors. The designer is expected to construct all the sceneries in a single shot on basis of a certain world view. He has to justify their existence and ensure that all of them observe a uniform style, represent innovative conceptions, and can satisfy certain requirements. An excellent oeuvre-d'art of scene design will survive repetitive inspections. The designer can depend on his outstanding skills and striking visual effects to attract the viewer's attention, while creative conceptions and fantastic ideas can give the viewers many inspirations. The meanings implied will enlighten the viewers to think more about the artwork itself, while rigorous thinking will ensure the integrity of the works and help to elevate it to a higher

level. In this sense, a designer has to be qualified in the following ways to produce outstanding scene design works.

a. Well-trained in Drawing

Paintings can always impress people in a visual way. A designer can neither design nor innovate unless he can illustrate out what he thinks and sees at ease. It requires years of practice and solid trainings to accomplish outstanding works.

b. Innovative Concepts

A designer cannot survive fierce competitions in the industry solely depending on realist sketches. In addtion to solid trainings in

IV. What Categories are Scene Design Works Divided into?

a. Historical Approach to Categorize the Scene Design works

Based on historical considerations, scene design works can be divided into two categories: one refers to artistic drawings. Such works are an independent piece of oeuvre-d'art itself and do not need to serve other media. This category includes landscape paintings, scene design works and scene illustration works, etc. Most works are drawings, including oil paintings and watercolor paintings in the West and ink paintings in the East. Even though artists from different regions will employ different expressive approaches and have different creative inspirations, all scene designers are actually trying to voice their personal feelings through atmosphere and effects of the finish.

"Seek the Gospel in Autumn Mountain" by Ju Ran

"Autumn Trees and Mountain" by Gong Xian

"The Avenue at Middelharnis" by Meindert Hobbema

"The Windmill at Wijk bjj Duurstede" by Jacob Izaaksoon van Ruisdael

© Ford

ford ENDEAVOUR

The other category encompasses design works of practical meanings, such as illustrations in the book, stage setting, etc. This category is supposed to be at service of the contents and foreground, helping to facilitate understanding, enhance atmosphere and highlight subjects. Scene design is applied in more and more areas with the development in the industry, including game, movie, animation, in addition to advertising, poster, and matte painting. Nowadays, the boundary between these two categories of works have become less visible. Artistic paintings are active in the design profession, serving as a catalyst to the most primitive artistic inspirations, while design works of practical meanings can be considered as an emerging art. Illustration works of outstanding quality have become treasured collections in the galleries.

Except this historical approach, scene design works can be divided in a more elaborate way based on theme and subject.

Matte painting for Ford ENDEAVOUR Advertisements

CG illustration exhibition at LeewiArt

© Ford

ford ENDEAVOUR

Matte painting for Ford ENDEAVOUR Advertisements

b. How Are the Scene Design Works Categorized in This Book?

Many theoretical textbooks tend to categorize scene design works into "indoor scene," "outdoor scene," and "blend of indoor and outdoor scene." However, such a categorization is subject to considerable limitations. Special spaces such as "submarine world" and "underground cavern" falls into none of the aforementioned categories. Thus, in addition to this approach, there are also other ways of categorization. For example, the works can be divided into fantasy, reality and other categories based on the subjects. This book adopts a categorization approach which divides the works into two kinds on basis of perspective, composition and expressive modes: one is "landscape," while the other is "environment." The former is more adaquate to illustrate a vast space, using depth of field to give full expression to the splendor. The latter category has a better performance to depicting the details and features of particular objects in the space, capturing the warmth and delicacy of a given scene while highlighting the details.

The beauty of such a categorization is mainly reflected in the following aspects: this approach can cover a wider range of works due to its departure from specific generalization of certain phenomena. No matter what category a given piece of works belongs to, the most important thing is how the works can impress the viewer. Scene design works also follow this rule. The look and effects a scene represents should help to make the works more impressive.

Based on years of experience, I believe that urban constructions present a relatively special subject, because this subject can be handled both as landscape and environment. Moreover, in illustrating urban constructions, the designer is required to have outstanding skills in dealing with perspective and structure. Therefore, I have decided to use a separate chapter to talk about urban constructions in this book.

In addition, "still props in the scene" constitute an integral component in environment works. In addition to highlighting the atmosphere, this element can also work to illustrate the splendid details, which explains why designers have started to pay more attention to it in recent years. Still props deserve meticulous explanations both in the sense of concepts and ideas and in the sense of drawing skills. Thus, we will deal with this topic in a separate chapter in this book.

Besides the aforementioned categorization approaches, we can go further to divide scene design works into those intended to reproduce real scenes but somewhat incorporating a small amount of atmosphere construction, and those mainly intended to highlight the atmosphere. The former category is mainly targeted at concrete scenes, including landscape works and environment works which are divided on basis of perspective and composition. The latter category is more focused on atmosphere construction. The designer is expected to switch his attention from depicting concrete sceneries to building up atmosphere. Some works would even illustrate certain sceneries in a suggestive way in order to achieve intensive atmosphere effects. We can decide on the final categorization of works by controling the relationship between "scenery depiction" and "atmosphere management." Therefore, we will use a separate chapter to approach this issue in this book.

A scene illustration featuring abstract styles

This scene illustration of abstract styles neglects the depiction of concrete objects in order to highlight the mysteries of the lane in the forest. What is noteworthy is that the designer should measure to what extent exaggeration along with abstract and uncommon elements is used in the illustration based on what the works are used for. The designer should take caution not to over-emphasize on "atmosphere," since works are generally targeted at the majority.

Chapter II

Basic Principles and Procedures for Scene Design

Overview

Overview

Generally speaking, scene design illustrations differ little from other categories of illustrations considering that the illustrating and designing process also involves concept development, subject selection, drafting, and elaboration. This category is neither as emotionally provocative as character-themed illustrations, nor intended for story-telling like scenario illustrations. Thus, in order to produce an outstanding scene design illustration, the designer has to give his work a nostalgic touch or a breath of freshness by elaborating on constitution and composition, instead of solely depending on atmosphere, spatial and structural elements. In addition, the designer has to make full use of some special techniques in order to enliven the lifeless scenery, present to the viewers a more powerful visual impact and leave them more room for imagination. It should be noted that there are established procedures which correspond with different categories of scene design illustrations, by following which the designer will find it easier in the illustrating process. This chapter will deal with different categories of scene design works one after another, exemplifying the varied illustrating procedures and presenting to the readers a relatively integral framework concerning scene design.

I. Concept Development for Themed Works and Non-themed Works

Concept development refers to the process to search for and build on the concept. As the initial phase in illustration, it determines where the designer heads for and where he ends. The designer is supposed to take many considerations, such as the subjects and content, objects and atmosphere as well as the illustration style and manipulation approaches. The designer should keep all these considerations in mind in every phase. Throughout the creation process, he is supposed to be guided by his reason.

When talking about concept development, we cannot skip over inspiration. "Inspiration" refers to a flashing sensation in the rational creation process. In this process, inspirations will pop up one after another. What the designer is supposed to do is to seize the inspirations in a timely way, incorporate them in his concepts, sorting out these sensational and accidental thoughts, and translating them into logical concepts and concrete configuration. All these are indispensable for the concept development process.

Generally speaking, scene design works can be divided into two categories: the commissioned category refers to those whose objectives are specific and topics are predetermined; the other category is non-commissioned work which is solely driven by inspiration.

When working on commissioned works, the designer is expected to fully observe the specific requirements from the clients. Objective-oriented, the creation process for this category is clearly-charted, and logically driven; the finish is generally well-developed. Commissioned works are largely used for commercial or practical use.

Non-commissioned work has nothing to do with specific requirements from clients. When doing this category, the designer will follow the call of his inspirations, and build on the blurry concepts and impressions. As both themes and concepts evolve from his gushing inspirations, the designer should always keep in mind where he originally intends to head for. Moreover, the designer should visualize the blurry concepts through logical reorganization and coordination. If the designer has failed to meet the requirements in this process, he is doomed to be haunted by myriad distractions and obstructions throughout the creative process, making the whole process more challenging.

"The monastery"

II. How to Create the Sense of Space in Scene Design

Scene designers need to take consideration of major objects and principal elements when deciding on the composition of the illustration. In this process, how to create the sense of space is a top concern. The designer needs to emulate the relationship between objects in the 3D space on a 2D plane, in order to create a sense of depth and gradation. In creating the sense of space, the designer should take good considerations of the following three points.

a. Precise Perspectives

In scene design, basic knowledge concerning the perspective subject is of high importance. One of the underlying principles is that objects nearby are larger than those afar. This principle is based on the perspective phenomenon that the closer the object is from the point of sight, the larger the object will look.

The most common defect in scene design is imprecise perspective. The "perspective" as mentioned here mostly refers to "perspective effects of configurative changes." Though these illustrations are targeted at viewers instead of artists and scholars, scenes illustrated should be all based on people's daily life and observation habits. Thus, if there is anything wrong with the perspective, a viewer without sharp eyes might also spot it. When the relationship between objects and their structures and composition have become more complicated, it becomes more difficult to deal with the perspective. We need to master these principles in order to avoid approaching this issue in a totally academic way, which will pose obstacles to the creative process.

b. Purifying Color and Matching Cold and Warm Colors

The suspended articles in the air have created special visual effects. Consequently, objects closer to the point of sight are relatively more clearer and warmer in color, while those farther from the point of sight are relatively less clear and warm in color.

c. Using the Changes in Depth of Field

Depth of field is a photographical concept, referring to the range of distances in object space for which object points are imaged with acceptable sharpness. In an illustration with depth of field, the artists can emulate the definition declination due to changes in distance. Objects closer to the focus will appear clearer, while those at a farther distance from the focus will become blurry, producing a sense of depth in the space.

Among the aforementioned three points, precise perspective effects constitute a basic requirement to create a sense of space. Meanwhile, color and depth are essential expressive languages for scene illustrations, which should be jointly applied in order to better illustrate the three-dimensional space. In this book, these two expressive languages are jointly termed as "atmosphere effect," which will be narrated in detail in Chapter III.

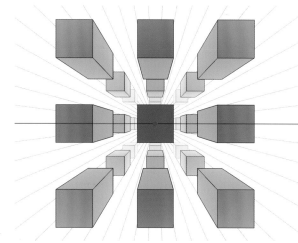

A parallel perspective plan

On the right is a plan featuring the parallel perspective, in which hexahedron has been applied to help illustrate the relations between different objects and stereo-imaging effects. The point of sight in the illustration is parallel with the objects, which will vertically vanish from the central point from near to far. Through the twenty-seven cubes are of identical sizes and equal distance in the space, the influence of perspective on the configurative changes and object relations has become evident. The perspective relationship is one of the primary concerns in composition of scene design illustrations.

An illustration featuring a strong sense of perspective

II. The Importance of Drafts

Some might confuse "drafts" with "initial scribbles." An impressive illustration does not only depend on the indispensable passions and inspirations in the production process. Rational preparations and planning in the pre-production phase are also of paramount significance. Many designers cannot hold back from picking up their pen the moment a blurry vision pops up in their mind. They would rush to put this illusion to paper and build upon this illusion. Actually, this is not an optimal choice. The designer should be quick to record his inspirations when they knock on the door. However, what the designers have recorded is actually incomplete, which should be better used as a reference rather than a determined draft intended for the formal production process. Drawing drafts is an important means to record the designers' inspirations and develop their concepts.

When inspirations sparkle in our mind, we should record them in a brief way. Later, we could experiment with different perspectives and different composition schemes to figure out which can better illustrate the theme or subject awaiting depiction. When working on the drafts, the designer is also supposed to search for relevant referential materials and incorporate them into his design concepts by making up for the incompletion and imperfection. Eventually, the designer will start to work on a complete draft to use as the formal starting point for the production process.

I have conducted comparative research. Well-crafted drafts might take more time in the initial phase, but promise a much smoother and quicker progression than the drafts less well-conceived. Due to inadequate preparation in the beginning, the latter category requires constant amendments and adjustments as a result from an obstructed flow in production. In addition, the finish will appear awkward and absurd. In some cases, ill-considered drafts are likely to jeopardize the blurry concepts at the initial phase of the production process, or the finish might differ from what the designer intends to illustrate in the very beginning.

Drafts for *"The Tracks in the Amusement Park on the Coast"*

Initial drafts for *"The Tracks in the Amusement Park on the Coas*

IV. Basic Procedure for Scene Design

Production of a scene design illustration involves a series of processes. However, this procedure is not determined, which means it is not necessary to follow every process in order to produce an illustration. Sometimes, certain processes can be integrated. For example, the designer might have determined the major objects to illustrate when deciding on the theme. Or, he might have finished the drafts when thinking about perspectives and composition. All these processes might differ to different designers in different projects. We only intend to present a general ideal approach to the readers while highlighting how some processes are carried out. The exact approach is as follows:

a. Deciding on the Theme

No matter it is commissioned illustration, or non-commissioned illustration, the designer should firstly decide on the theme, which should be based on research and inspirations. The theme determines what effects and scenery the illustration intends to demonstrate, what attitudes and emotions the designer desires to capture, and the atmosphere and meanings the illustration plans to convey. All these elements are involved in the initial phase of the overall production process.

b. Selecting Suitable Scenery and Atmosphere Based on the Theme

The designer should base on the predetermined theme to select appropriate scenery and atmosphere, which is essential to what effects the illustration eventually intends to demonstrate. As the paramount element in the illustration, scenery refers to the objects that exist in it. Atmosphere is supposed to convey certain emotions through well-considered manipulation of light and scenery. The designer should strive to construct special atmosphere to give voice to emotions through scenery in order to highlight the theme, which is actually a process to visualize the theme.

c. Selecting Suitable Perspective and Composition Approaches Based on the Theme

As to scene design illustrations, there is another element of essential importance to be determined, in addition to scenery and atmosphere — perspective and composition. As what needs to be illustrated in this category all exist in a space constructed, spatial configuration is of high significance to scene design illustrations. On the other hand, perspective and composition are fundamental to spatial configuration, which evidences their importance.

d. Drawing Drafts

In this stage, the designer is expected to work on the drafts based on the predetermined concepts, central connotations and themes to illustrate. What should be noted here is the integrity of composition in the illustration, configuration of key characteristics in the major objects and rough manipulation of the overall atmosphere.

Coloring and refining — a basic process in scene design

Elaborating on the details — a basic process in scene design

e. Coloring and Refining

The designer should start to color the drafts and decide on the overall hue and lighting effects. Color palette, color matching scheme, the quantity, positions and intensity of lighting sources all determine the style of the illustration. The dominant hue and dominant lighting source can help to enhance the atmosphere and determine where the designer heads for.

After deciding on the light and color elements, the designer should start to make adjustments to the sense of space and the relationship between different objects in the illustration. In this stage, the designer examines and refines the drafts in terms of the structure for major objects, perspective relationship, and sense of distance.

f. Elaborating on Details

In this process, the designer is expected to optimize the configurations of all the objects, and elaborate on the surroundings of the point of sight and details of the major objects. In this way, the designer can manage to highlight the gradation, enhance the expressive power and give prominence to the theme.

Elaboration on the configuration will affect the changes in light and color. The designer should build upon the complication and precision degree. In addition, he should take consideration of their mutual influences when working on the configuration and color palette.

g. Enhancing the Atmosphere

In this stage, the designer should work on the atmosphere elements to highlight the theme by examining and adjusting the overall picture until the illustration is completed. The atmosphere elements mentioned here is different from the atmosphere effects touched upon in the passages in earlier chapters. These effect elements that can function to elevate the theme include pouring rain, shrouding smoke and mists, and drifting blossoms. If painted earlier, these elements will affect the elaboration of the background, which determines that this job should be postponed to the last few stages.

All the aforementioned are the basic processes to produce scene design illustrations.

Atmosphere enhancement — a basic process in scene design

V. How to Discuss the Proposal with the Clients

Scene designers are generally more insistent on their personal style. Thus, it becomes a premise for the smooth completion of projects to unify the designers' concepts with those of the clients. In order to ensure a smooth progression, the designer should communicate and discuss with the clients in a constant way. However, over-frequent inspection and supervision will affect the designer making best use of their techniques. How can a designer manage to communicate with the clients in a correct and rational way, without diverting from the clients' concepts or being restrained? Generally speaking, a designer should communicate with his clients in the following four processes.

a. When the Designer Receives Commissions from the Clients

The designer is expected to familiarize the project requirements and plans, which are submitted by the clients. At this stage, it is necessary to have face-to-face communication with the clients over the project requirements, and decide on whether he can give full play to his creativity after understanding the clients' requirements.

b. When the Designer Is Working on the Drafts

In this process, the designer is supposed to draw the drafts based on the requirements and schemes of the given project. In the initial phase, the drafts might be quite inadequately crafted. However, the designer should try to experiment with as many concepts as possible. Generally speaking, for the same scene, he should draw at least three to four illustrations that are closely related to the theme. All these illustrations are supposed to feature varied perspectives, ambiences, as well as different climates and time periods, from which the clients can make a choice.

Drafts for the *"Decayed Temple Relics"* Project

c. When the Designer Is Elaborating on the Drafts

In this stage, the designer will start to elaborate on one or two drafts that the client has selected. Initial efforts should be focused on the color palette, with ambience and scenery roughly handled. When submitted to the clients, the designer can use some referential photos or illustrations of similar styles to enable the clients to have a better understanding.

d. When the Designer Has Decided on a Certain Proposal

In this process, the client must have chosen his favorite illustration and come up with some suggestions for revision. After confirming with the client the revised scheme, the designer can start to elaborate on the illustrations. At this stage, the style and design concept is supposed to be basically determined, leaving little necessity for revision. However, the designer can still compare notes with the clients throughout the later phases until the illustration is finished.

{ Tip }

If the client is not satisfied with any illustration from those that are presented to him for the first time, it indicates that your personal style and design concept are in contradiction with the commission to a considerable extent. If so, the designer is advised to make changes to his concepts.

Elaborating on the color and details of the selected proposals

VI. Tools and Software Programmes That Might Be Used in the Later Implementation Process

Scene design should not be confused with simple scene illustration, considering the first category is relatively diversified due to its association with design. Therefore, diverse applications of tools and software will be favorable for design creation and effect presentation.

Categories of Illustration	Advantages	Application Fields	Common Tools and Softwares
2D Illustration	Outstanding performance in atmosphere construction like traditional painting; helping to capture and document the inspirations in a swift manner	Applying to the initial draft design, post-production and atmosphere enhancement	Painter/ Photoshop
3D Illustration	Able to illustrate the concrete objects in the scene in a more elaborate way; facilitating realistic shading, precise perspective, and depth of field effects	Interior or exterior architectural scenes, scenes mainly featuring close shot and medium shot, scenes requiring dedicate and realistic painting, small-scale scenery and props in the environment illustration	3DS MAX/MAYA/ Softimage VUE (Those tailored for scene design)
Blend of 2D and 3D Illustrations	Counterbalancing the flaws of 3D production software by reducing the production process and those of the 2D software by strengthening the perspective, lighting effects and sense of space; incorporating the advantages of the aforementioned software	Applying to all kinds of scene design illustrations	All those mentioned above

Elaborate on the determined scheme until it is finished

Chapter III
Trainings in Scene Design

A. Landscape

Overview

Gallery

A. Landscape

Overview

"Landscape" generally refers to scenes featuring wide view and breath-taking magnificence. It can be natural scenery or an architectural complex in real life, or the fantasy world as a crystallization of man's imagination. No matter what is to be depicted, landscape works should impress people with their magnificence and splendor. The structure can be so towering to pierce into the sky, or so abysmal to be seemingly bottomless; it can be so vast to extend to where sky and land meet, or so spacious that all the sceneries unfold before the viewers' eye. There are several distinctive features with landscape works: a wide field of view, an emotionally powerful atmosphere and a striking visual effect. Owing to these features, such works are applied in wide-ranging areas. In addition to landscape illustrations and landscape paintings, this category can also be used for large scenes, commanding atmosphere, geomorphologic maps in games and movies, or the background in advertisements and posters.

I. Concept Development

The designer should decide on the primary theme when working on landscape works. He has to take serious thoughts over what he intends to give full expression to through his works beyond magnificence — whether it is desolation, destruction, noises, or prosperity. All these factors should be determined after serious consideration. Only by incorporating these elements could the designer breathe life into his works. Otherwise, his works will turn out to be nothing more than a picture of landscape.

After deciding on the primary theme, the designer should start to think about environmental factors that could help to demonstrate the theme. These factors include landform, seasons, climate, etc. Among these factors, the designer should select those that are more closely related to the theme of the given works, and start to hunt for relevant reference materials. Generally speaking, the references come from photography works, which can inspire us in different ways. For example, the winding hills enveloped by morning fogs, waves of flowers glittering in the sunshine at noon, rainforest shrouded in gloominess in the evening, or the borderless grassland on a summer afternoon. We can locate the elements we are looking for in these photos and construct the desired environment.

{ Tip }

After deciding on a certain theme, a visual image will form up in the designers' mind. Many designers are likely to be so consumed with this image that they will use this image to look for relevant references; this might pose restrictions for the later process. In fact, in the search for references, the designer should follow his intuition, instead of being restrained by obscure illusions in his mind, because there is a high possibility that this illusion might not lead to an optimal result. This can only be achieved on the basis of a comprehensive understanding of the subject itself.

References for landscape works

II. Basic Composition and Drafts

What is most important about emulating the wide-angle effects is to simulate the distortions at the edge of the image.

Wide-angle is commonly used in landscape works, because this angle of view will enhance the sense of depth for the space. A relatively long depth of field can ensure that objects before or behind the major objects can be clearly reproduced in the illustration, capturing the entire scenery by maximizing the entire scenery and enhancing a sense of magnificence. Considering the relationship between the scenery and the line of sight, wide angle and horizontal view are generally incorporated for optimal effects. The combination of wide angle and worm's-eye view is to emulate the effects in which the viewer looks up from a lower position. This perspective is generally employed to illustrate towering architecture or natural formation, making the main objects more powerful. Such illustrations will permeate with a sense of solemnity, leaving the viewers awe-stricken. The larger the angle of elevation is, the more tensed and pressed the viewers are supposed to feel, and the more threatening the main objects will seem to be.

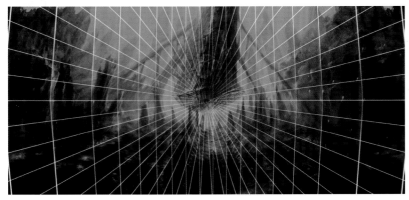

The horizontal wide-angle only possesses one vanishing point located on the horizon which is positioned in the center of the illustration at the same height with the viewer's eyes. This perspective applies to the occasions when a considerable number of objects are intended to be depicted.

A landscape illustration using the horizontal wide-angle

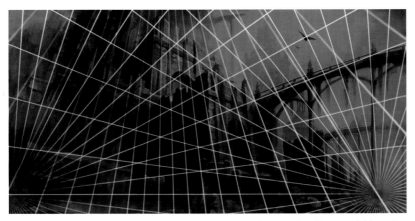

The referential perspective rays demonstrating worm's-eye level perspective; the two vanishing points are respectively located on the left and right sides of the illustration, which effectively highlights the magnificence of the large objects at near distance, such as skyscrapers and lofty mountains.

A landscape illustration featuring worm's-eye view and wide angle

Bird's-eye view wide angle refers to the practice which positions the viewer's eyes in a high location, observing the entire scenery like a flying bird. Such a perspective applies to the occasion in which a landform of considerable vastness or a panoramic view of a special building is intended to be presented. The bird's-eye view is suitable for giving a whole picture of where the story takes place. Such illustrations can be drawn using one-point perspective, two-point perspective or three-point perspective, while one-point perspective is the most commonly used.

One-point perspective ray in a bird's-eye-view wide-angle illustration for reference; the vanishing point is located on the horizon. This perspective best applies to the general plan to present a panoramic view.

A landscape illustration featuring a bird's-eye view wide angle

In addition to the three perspectives mentioned in the former chapters, some landscape illustrations highlighting the sense of magnificence feature a composition approach of non-wide-angle horizontal view. Using this approach, the designer generally makes use of the contrast between objects of different sizes to create a sense of magnificence. Without the wide-angle effects, horizontal view by itself is seldom used in the landscape illustration due to inadequate effect.

After selecting an ideal perspective for the composition, the designer generally will sketch out some objects in a quick way. Considering the environmental factors and subjects to be depicted, they should try different ways to place objects for an optimal scheme. As shown in the following example, the designer doesn't decide on the landform and scenery until numerous revisions have been made.

A rushed sketch, which contains all kinds of elements featuring long shot, close shot and medium shot

A second rushed sketch in which the relationship between close-shot landform and long-shot objects, as well as the configuration of the land have been changed

A third rushed sketch, in which landform and objects have been modified

III. Special Techniques for Landscape Illustrations

a. Lighting Effects

In addition to perspective and composition, lighting is another essential element for landscape illustrations. How many lighting sources are positioned, how strong they are, and where to place them are all significant considerations for later processes. After all, a world without light is nothing more than a cluster of darkness. In the drafting process, the designer can try to change the lighting sources in different ways for the best lighting effect.

Lighting effect for outdoor scenery glittering in mid-day sunshine

Lighting effect for outdoor scenery shrouded in darkness at night

Lighting effect for outdoor scenery glittering in the sunshine in the afternoon

Lighting effect for outdoor scenery gilded with twilight

b. Atmosphere Effects

There is another important factor that a designer is supposed to consider in the designing process, which is "atmosphere effect." This factor determines the sense of space for the entire illustration as well as the gradation and depth relations between different objects.

The "atmosphere effect" mentioned here actually refers to the phenomenon that dirt and pollutants flowing in the air will influence the visibility range. The broader a given space is, the more pollutants and dirt there are in the air, and the more obvious the blocking effect is. Thus, the objects will seem a little foggy to the viewers.

The "atmosphere effect" applies to all kinds of landscape illustrations. It is an important factor to create the depth of field and gradation effects in the picture, making the scenery more real to the viewers. This is essential to landscape illustrations, as it is an integral element to highlight the sense of magnificence. Due to the vastness of space and the complexity of scenery, the details do not matter so much. The overall atmosphere is what the designer is supposed to focus on.

Gradation relations between different objects in the canyon

Gradation relations between different objects have changed with the "atmosphere effect."

Gradation relations between medium-shot peaks and long-shot mountains

Gradation relations between different objects have changed with the "atmosphere effect."

IV. Case Studies

a. *Sea*

We will take the example to explain how to employ wide-angle horizontal view in landscape illustrations.

❶ Concept Development

This illustration is actually inspired by a documentary on coral reefs. When watching this documentary, I was marveled by the emerald sea and crystal blue sky, which made me pick up the pen and create this illustration. Sky and sea usually impress people with their vastness. Thus, both are ideal subjects for landscape illustrations. Featuring a fantasy style, such illustrations are different from ordinary scenery illustrations to a considerable extent. The highlight of this "fantasy" illustration is the "castle on the sea" which is located between the land and the coral reefs. This special castle has added radiance to the originally prosaic sight.

To create an impressive oeuvre-d'art, it requires more than inspirations and years of practice. The designer is also supposed to spend a large quantity of time in thinking and analyzing activities in the concept development process in order to make his works more visually appealing to the viewers.

"Sea"

❷ Composition

In order to give full expression to the sense of vastness, low-level horizontal view has been employed. The horizon where sky and land meet is situated higher than the center of the illustration. Consequently, the visibility range will be broadened. This approach is different from the perspective effect used to depict close-shot or near-shot sea surface. In the latter category a bird's-eye view is usually applied. The designer has positioned the horizon at the upper half of the illustration, which gives a perfect perspective to depict the coral reefs and the constructions on the sea. As this illustration is also concerned with natural scenery in real life, the designer can leave alone the fantasy elements when working on the drafts to ensure the precision of the perspective effects. However, the designer should start to consider where to place them and adjust the wide-angle composition of the background accordingly.

Referential landscape illustration of perspective effects

❸ Elaborating on the Drafts

After adjusting the sizes and locations of sky, sea, reefs and land, the designer should focus on capturing the distinctive features of different elements. At this stage, it is suggested that the designer should refer to some scenery photos of similar perspectives, and take note of details such as where the land, reefs and land meet. How to deal with these details really matters. If roughly-done, the entire illustration will end in chaos, where every element exists independently instead of being integrated with each other to become a whole. At this stage, the designer is expected to take more consideration of the credibility while making preparations to elaborate on the illustration in the later process. For example, observed from this perspective, reefs mostly nestle in shallow waters, where there are no raging waves. Where the land and sea meet is not sand, so the waves will turn into sprays when throwing themselves upon rocky cliffs. This concept has incorporated both the static and dynamic elements for a rich variety of sceneries. Massive clouds weigh down over the sea, which makes a distinction of where the sea and sky meet and diversifies the background for the constructions in the sea.

Draft

❹ Adjustments in the Drawing Process

In this stage, the designer will be confronted with some challenges. At the drafting stage, there is no way to make an accurate estimation of the location of the main construction. Without corresponding adjustments, the center of the illustration will look a little jammed when the constructions are added. Therefore, I have moved the main construction to the left, introduced some new elements to the left, and adjusted the wide-angle, so as to broaden the visual range and reducing the sense of crowdedness in the illustration without changing the estimated composition.

Elaborate on the characteristics of the scenery to make it easier for the later processes

Adjust to wide-angle composition

Add relevant objects to give emphasis to the theme, and make up for the defects in composition

⑤ Add Objects to Diversify the Sceneries

Considering the sky and water in the background, I have chosen to depict a castle with fountains flowing from its dome for a coherent atmosphere in the illustration. This fantasy element will change the originally dull world view. As the tranquil sea seems a little boring here, we could use the construction and several reefs to create a contrast and divide the sea into two gradations. Such an approach will reject the original insipidity, and add radiance to the castle. After that, I have added the islands suspending in the air and stone pagoda to enhance the fantasy atmosphere.

At this stage, the sea surface on the left seems a little monotonous. Therefore, I have added a stone pagoda at near shot in the left, which chimes in concert with the one on the seashore on the right and the one in the long shot. Crowning the major construction and connected with each other with iron chains, the three pagodas form up a triangle when observed from the sky. At this stage, the illustration is flawless both in terms of composition and content. Three stone pagodas are erected on the sea, land and reefs respectively, which is in consistence with the theme of the illustration. The three pagodas point to the major construction, creating a sense of perspective which can add to the magnificence of the illustration. Some designs of unique concepts have added radiance to each other, further highlighting the fantasy theme.

❻ Color Management

In the initial design stage, the designer should be focused on a rational concept while taking good consideration of how to position and configure different elements. In order to capture the vanishing inspirations, a rough palette is enough. But when the designer starts to decide on various design elements, color management should be

In the aerial view, it can be seen that the constructions, including the castle, have formed up a triangle.

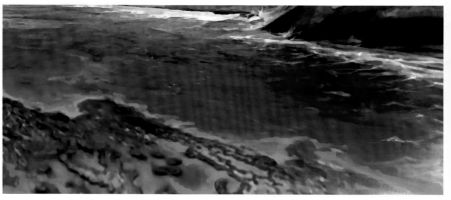

Work on the texture and details of sea surface

prioritized. In illustrating emerald sea and blue sky, the first thing to do is to purify the color. In order to give a breath of warmth to the illustration which is dominated by cold blue, we should increase the proportion of warm colors by adding relatively purified yellow to the construction, and apply purple in the dark spots to incorporate blue and yellow in a more subtle way.

❼ Work on the Texture of Details

As a dominant element in the illustration, sea has also acted as its inspiration. A highlight for this illustration is how the texture of the sea is presented. Belonging to the landscape category, this illustration will not experience a considerable improvement in quality with details added to the long-shot scenery. Thus, capturing the most distinctive features of the long-shot elements will turn out to be more rewarding. Based on the rise and fall of different landforms, we should add the giant reflections of the towering cliffs when handling the waters bordering the cliffs on the land, in addition to the sprays. Smashed by the waves, the reflections will become a little difficult to identify. All these approaches will enhance the dynamics of the seawater. In addition, the waters cradling the reefs in the shallow sea will take on a hue of special emerald due to its unique location when bathed in the sunshine.

❽ Elaborate on the Details

In order to enhance the sense of gradation, the designer should add details from far to near. The detailing effects are aimed at enriching the sceneries and adding dramas. New highlights are only to be added on the basis that there is not any flaw with the lighting and configurations effects. These highlights should be relatively integral elements which can relate to and add radiance to the major objects, such as the stone pagoda on the reefs. When dealing with the object closest to the viewer's eyes, I have added green vines on the surface of the pagoda to give a sense of history. Besides, flowing waters have been introduced to give full expression of the dynamics and liveliness. If we had chosen the cracks in the stone surface to elaborate on, it would not have helped to improve the quality of the illustration either in terms of visual effect or meanings. Therefore, we should keep the whole picture in mind when working on the details and make the best choices.

After depicting all the objects, we should add facula, intensify the lighting effects, strengthen the foggy effects and incorporate a few small elements such as flying birds to enhance the atmosphere. A fantasy landscape illustration is finally completed.

How much effort to spend on the details depends on the designer's personal concept and style. According to my personal experience, there is no need to go further if desired effects for atmosphere and details have been achieved. Whether to work further on the illustration to make it photo-like is determined by the artist's personal style and the purpose this illustration is used for.

Add details to the building

Add atmosphere elements and make adjustments just before the illustration is finished

b. *Mountains and Waters*

We will take the example of "Mountains and Waters" to give a brief introduction to how bird's-eye view illustrations are produced.

This bird's-eye view wide-angle landscape illustration draws inspirations from Chinese landscape and relics of temples. In the former passages, I have mentioned that bird's-eye view illustrations is the best choices to present a panoramic view of massive landform and special architectural complex. This oeuvre-d'art can exemplify the beauty of the bird's-eye-view landscape illustration.

❶ Concept Development

Illustrations on ancient temples and winding mountains featuring the Chinese style are very common in this profession. Most works will observe the composition and perspective principles in typical Chinese landscape paintings which would feature a suggestive style. This approach applies to the depiction of drifting and enveloping clouds and mists, but can neither highlight the precipitousness of cliffs nor enhance the sense of depth and the visual impacts. All these aforementioned problems can be avoided by using the bird's-eye view wide angle.

"Mountains and Waters"

Draft based on composition

Work on the details and add more objects

Add atmosphere elements, and make adjustments before the illustration is finished

❷ Composition

This illustration largely follows the same basic processes and key considerations with *Sea*, which is employed as an example in the passages concerned with wide-angle landscape illustrations. What differs is that this illustration features a powerful sense of depth in composition and prioritizes structural perspective. In the first place, the designer should work on concept development. This perspective is uncommon in daily life. But standing on the roof of skyscraper to look down at the buildings below can help the designer to find inspiration. It is advised to search for this kind of photo for reference — designers can imagine high buildings as peaks and draw drafts based on the perspective relations in the photos.

❸ Elaborate on the Details

The designer is supposed to pay attention to perspectives as well as ensure a clear structure and relationship when adding details to the ancient construction and cliffs on the drafts. Though in bird's-eye view, peaks rise over peaks, screening the horizon and sky, the designer still has to erase unnecessary mountains and peaks after deciding on the space for the major construction, so as to leave more space for the long-shot objects and ensure a sense of flowing air. Considering this, the designer should apply light blue to distant mountains and use the transfiguration approach featuring "fish-eye view" wide angle to reveal a glimpse of sky.

This illustration has adopted an unconventional perspective to achieve impressive effects: forested mountains and emerald water, mysterious clouds and mists, cliff peaks rising one higher than another all require portraying. The designer will find this category of illustrations more challenging, because it involves more considerations. However, this category differs little from the former category in terms of composition, so I'll leave out reptitive iutroductions What needs to be emphasized is that in order to come up with more innovative works, it's worthwhile to do some rational thinkings before picking up the pen.

Summary

Trainings in landscape illustrations will help to develop skills to deal with multiple-layer perspective and multiple-perspective scenery in a broad visual range, and manage the sense of depth and atmosphere effects in long-shot landscape illustrations to highlight a sense of magnificence.

It requires flames of inspirations and industrious efforts in concept development in order to enable the viewers to feel impressed or awed by the world the designer attempts to construct. Thus, the designer must have outstanding skills to manage landscape illustrations. Though more challenging, this category is what a scene designer must deal with, and what one needs to prove personal skills and creativity.

As this category involves a wide range of objects, the designer needs to take consideration of the credibility and coherence in every process. These considerations include a variety of design elements such as structure, perspective, lighting and shadow. In order to come up with an integral and vivid fantasy world, the designer needs to keep the overall atmosphere in mind when attending to every detil.

Gallery

The Yellow River

Software: Painter

The designer has employed a
wide-angle horizontal view to
illustrate the magnificence and
splendor of the Hukou Waterfalls on
the Yellow River.

Cliffs

Software: Painter

The designer uses reddish lava to enrich the palette, and applies lighting effects to highlight the sense of depth in illustrating the winding canyon and cavern in this bird's-eye view illustration.

Mount Everest

Software: Painter

The designer uses the horizontal view to illustrate the precipitous and towering Mount Everest. Besides, the Marnyi Stones have been added in the close shot to enhance the atmosphere by exemplifying Tibetan cultural heritage.

The Stadium

Software: Painter \ Photoshop\ 3DS MAX

Based on the simple model developed using 3DS MAX, the designer has drawn a bird's-eye illustration of the urban architecture. This method will be explained in detail in the following chapters. The illustration depicts the last moment before the football game starts in the twilight.

B. Environment

Overview

Gallery

B. Environment

Overview

Environment illustrations encompass a rich variety of works. This category is actually defined in dichotomy to landscape illustrations. All the scene design works with a relatively restricted visual range and a large proportion of close-shot or medium shot objects belong to environment illustrations. The subjects can be a natural or artificial scenery on a small scale, such as relics and remains, towns and streets, and the interior of certain buildings. This category of illustrations can be used as components for landscape illustrations, background for movie and drama, structural sketch of architecture, in addition to acting as independent scene illustrations or paintings.

In contrast to landscape illustrations, environment illustrations prioritize atmosphere construction and detailed presentation. Without awe-inspiring perspectives, the overall atmosphere is no longer the top concern. As the viewers have been brought closer to the objects in the illustration, how the designer deals with details has become a highlight. Coupled with the overarching atmosphere, the works will consequently obtain a breath of vividness.

{ Tip }

This approach only applies to the occasion when the atmosphere has been predetermined. On such occasions, the designer can decide on the theme in the first place, and consider what elements to include in the illustration later. However, if they are initially aimed at illustrating certain sceneries and then decide on what meanings and atmosphere needs to infuse into the illustration, the designer should approach in the same way as creating landscape illustrations.

I. Concept Development

The designer is supposed to decide on the subject and atmosphere in the initial phase when working on environment illustrations, which is the same with the landscape illustrations. The only difference is that the subjects to be depicted have changed with the shifts in perspective. The sense of vastness is out of tune with environment illustrations. Instead, this category is the optimal choice to present atmospheres such as warmth, mystery, inaccessibility and congestion.

After deciding on the subject, the designer should start to search for referential materials, which will be less challenging than in landscape illustrations. Because with a smaller space and a closer perspective, the designer will feel less restrained in selecting varied locations to demonstrate the same theme based on his personal preference. Take the "sense of warmth" for example. In order to build up this atmosphere, the designer can portray a corner in the room at night, where the glow of a fireplace blankets the sofa before it, incorporating warm colors with common furnishings in daily life; or they can depict the countryside in the afternoon, where drifting smoke rises from the chimney on the roof. Though these two illustrations are concerned with different subjects, both exude similar atmosphere. Thus, the designer needs to think further to decide on which subject to choose.

II. Basic Composition and Drafts

We have mentioned earlier that designers will find themselves less restrained in scenes and plots when working on environment illustrations. Though the space to be depicted has become smaller, there is more room for the designer to give voice to his imagination. As the designer does not need to follow definite rules as in landscape illustrations, he can refer to diversified composition approaches. If we really want to generalize some common points that all the illustrations of this category share, it is that designers should attach high values to the choice of perspective and use of space.

Examples of environment illustrations

a. Choice of Perspectives

Choice of perspective refers to the process in which the position of the viewer's eyes is located. This location affects the sense of depth and visual impact of the illustration as well as the major objects intended to be presented. Scene design works actually take advantage of perspective to lead the viewer's eyes.

Take the illustrations on the right for example. The first one is intended to illustrate the panoramic view of the scenery, while the other four depict the same object from different perspectives. The point of sight can be placed on the enormous window of the building. In such a case, the warm lights cast from the window illuminates the ground, radiating with a sense of tranquility and gentleness along with the starry sky in the distance. Or the designer can shift the point of sight to the facade of the building. If so, the lake glittering in the moonlight is undisturbed, looking like a mirror reflecting the solid walls of the castle; the flourishing grass bordering the lake waves gently in the breeze, exuding a tranquil and harmonious atmosphere. When the point of sight has been positioned at the front door of the building, strong lights from indoors gilded the winding stairs and towering walls, imparting a sense of mystery. Or, the designer can elevate the point of sight to look up at the starry night, and create a serene and refreshing night by applying cold color as the dominant hue. Even with the subject unchanged, the theme and atmosphere might experience considerable changes with the shifting of point of sight. Thus, the most essential thing about environment illustrations is to find the ideal position of the point of sight.

As to the same scenery, where to place the point of view will determine what atmosphere the illustration creates. The series on the right exemplify how scenery can be approached from different perspectives.

b. Use of Space

Use of space refers to how and where all the objects are placed in the illustration in the initial phase of drafting. In environment illustrations, objects are closer to each other. Moreover, the designer could only draw a limited number of objects in this category of illustrations. Therefore, it is essential to ensure a rational relationship and a sense of gradation in determining the positions of these objects, so that the viewers will not find that certain objects do not belong to where they are placed. In this sense, how to use and manage the space has become very important.

The viewers can identify three gradations in the illustration: the close-shot "stone statue," the medium-shot "construction" and the long-shot "mountains." In this environment illustration, long-shot objects only occupy a small proportion, and function to enhance the depth of field and visually enlarge the distance between different objects. There are many close-shot and medium-shot objects in the illustration. Thus, it is important for the designer to take good consideration to determine how to give prominence to major objects without blocking the objects at the back or jeopardizing the overall structure and composition.

Take note of how to ensure the legitimacy of the composition

A major object is an indispensable element in environment illustrations

III. Techniques for Environment Illustrations

There is a considerable disparity between landscape illustrations and environment illustrations. In the former category, no matter what the atmosphere is, the sense of magnificence is an essential element due to the vastness of visual range. Thus, any object in landscape illustrations should be intended to highlight the sense of magnificence.

Take *Sea* as an example. The major object in this illustration is the castle offshore, while its overarching theme is the vastness of the emerald sea and blue sky — the castle in the center is just an element to highlight the theme. The theme will stay unchanged even without the castle.

Take the following illustration as another example. The illustration depicts a giant construction rising from the sea, demonstrating the sense of magnificence of the sea under a supernatural condition. Without the eye-catching "special" elements, the illustration will be reduced to an ordinary paysage painting which has lost the intensity of the atmosphere and changed the theme. However, the sense of vastness and magnificence still remain.

This sense of vastness and magnificence is a defining feature but eternal priority in landscape illustrations, while environment illustrations are concerned with depicting a limited number of objects in a space of limited size. In addition to demonstrating a certain atmosphere, this category of illustrations is mainly focused on certain objects. In such illustrations, major objects are indispensable.

In the environment illustrations themed on sea scenery, the works will be reduced to nothing when major objects such as shore, reefs and islands are erased.

Therefore, in environment illustrations, the designer is supposed to decide on the major objects to accord with the theme, which is one of the significant processes. Generally speaking, other objects should be positioned to crown the major objects. In terms of composition, major objects should be assigned to a prominent position in the illustration; moreover, corresponding adjustments should be made to other objects in terms of details, gradation, and depth of field.

A common approach to environment illustrations is: place the major objects in a prominent position, add details to them, give them optimal lighting effects, and design other objects to add radiance to major objects. In this way, the designer is able to produce a scene design oeuvre-d'art featuring a remarkable sense of gradation and clear-cut theme. In dealing with the gradation effects and depth of field, the designer should take good consideration of detail management and incorporate the "atmosphere effect" mentioned in the former chapter, which will help to achieve better results.

Landscape illustrations mainly focus on the sense of vastness and magnificence due to their distinctive characteristics in composition and scenery elements

The landscape illustrations will still exude a sense of vastness and magnificence even without some significant elements and effects

IV. Differences between Wide-angle Environment Illustrations and Landscape Illustrations

Diversity is a defining feature for outstanding oeuvres. In long-shot landscape illustrations, close-shot objects can be used to contrast with long-shot objects in terms of proportion, spatial relation and detail management to enhance the sense of gradation without stealing thunder from the long-shot major objects. In addition, the designer can go further to integrate all objects through uniform configuration to highlight the sense of wholeness and help demonstrate the overarching theme. It is the same with environment illustrations. Adding some long-shot objects as background will assist in enriching the illustration by highlighting the contrast and enhancing the sense of gradation. However, what should be noted is that the designer should control the proportion of the long-shot objects. Poorly managed, the overall atmosphere and the overarching theme predetermined might be affected.

Viewers can identify the category of works by examining the scale of space and the distribution of objects. On the other side, the designer needs to develop his concept and determine the category of works based on what message to deliver, what objects to illustrate and what the illustration is used for.

The work on the right is an example of wide-angle environment illustration. Take note of its difference from landscape illustrations.

The illustration below is intended as a Matte Painting resolution chart, which I did for an automobile advertisement. In the center of the illustration there will be a car soaring from afar and stopped in the very front of the camera. Due to the nature of the product and the restrains by the size of the advertisement, this illustration is designed as a wide-angle landscape illustration. In this illustration, the camera is targeted at the seashore, with flourishing forests on one side and surging waters on the other side. For such subjects, landscape illustrations seems to be a better choice; however, this illustration is not just intended as an ordinary scene design painting, it will be used as the background to give prominence to the product. As the highlight of the illustration must be the product itself, the environment illustration should be considered. Therefore, I worked on the illustration in the following way: I use the relatively limited space on the right to illustrate the coastline, and enhance the sense of depth by taking advantage of the sky and the horizon to broaden the distances between different objects. In addition, I have used the relatively large space a little left to the center to depict the close-shot forests and land. Though a wide-angle landscape is to be depicted, I still choose the typical approach applied in environment illustrations, which is more suitable for detail management.

V. Case Study

a. *The Lantern Street*

We will take *The Lantern Street* as an example to demonstrate how environment illustrations are produced.

❶ Concept Development

This illustration is intended to depict the lanterns on an antique street. A relatively conventional horizontal view has been applied to highlight the sense of depth of the street. Because this perspective can enable the viewers to have a panoramic view of the street to the largest extent, it is commonly used in illustrations on streets and buildings. In contrast to conventional composition and perspective, the illustration still features something unconventional. I have set the time for afternoon with plentiful sunshine, which does not seem a good time to illustrate lantern lights at the first look. However, the illustration has become more interesting as a result, instead of being reduced to an ordinary night scenery of streets without any highlight. The difference between scene design illustrations and traditional paysage paintings lie in how innovative the artist is. The illustration itself might not be concerned with fantasy subjects, but should be at least innovative. As long as it is innovative, an illustration on earthly subjects can still impress the viewers visually and emotionally.

"The Lantern Street"

❷ Composition

The designer should start with the sketch by observing the predetermined perspective. In this illustration, the point of sight has been placed a little to the left to give different proportions to streets on the left and right. All these are intended to make preparation for determining the priority status for different objects. After making decisions on the composition and perspective, the designer should genevally sketch out the lighting and shadow effects. As the time is set for the afternoon, the rays of sunshine should be a little tilted. The lighting source is placed on the right of the illustration. In such a way, the street on the left side which dominates a larger part in the illustration consequently becomes clear and well-illuminated. There are two reasons for this approach:

★ Balance the Priority Status

The element that occupies the majority of the illustration is generally its focus (such as the street on the left side in this illustration). It requires more lighting effects to help depict the details. The street on the right side takes up a smaller space and is cast in darker shadow to give prominence to the focus of the illustration.

★ Balance the Sense of Weight

Dark color gives a sense of weight, while light color is associated with a sense of lightness. If we have gone the other way by assigning large clusters of dark color to the left side of the illustration, the balance will be jeopardized, causing a visual sense of inconsistency.

{ Tip }

The sunshine is a little glaring in the afternoon. In such strong sunlight, the light and shadow effects will be highly evident, which means that shadows at this time will clearly capture the silhouette of the objects. The more complicated the way the objects are structured, the more complicated the lighting effects are. A profound understanding of the relationship between light and shadow, and a precise configuration of the objects' structure are top concerns for scene designers. Neglecting these factors will result in mountains of trouble in the later processes.

Pay attention to the lighting effects and the precision of perspective effects while working on the drafts.

Perspectives for reference

❸ Consideration of Lighting Effects and Depiction Work

The sky in the upper part of the illustration seems too spacious. I had considered elevating the heights of the lining constructions as a solution. However, increasing their heights will also cause changes to the lighting effects, which is in conflict with my original plan. Thus, I finally gave up this approach. Later, I have referred to the ceiling and roof window of the ancient railway stations by blocking the space over the street. Consequently, there will be basically no change to the lighting effects except a reduction in amount of light. In addition, the lining constructions have become more integrated. Considering all these beauties, I have decided to adopt this approach.

❹ Color Palette

Considering that the lanterns added later will radiate with a yellow halo, I have selected blue as the dominant hue. In order to highlight the sunlight rays and strike at a balance between warm color and cold color, I have greyed the illuminated surface of the building accordingly.

In environment illustrations, if the objects are integral and uniform, evenly distributed, the color palette should not be too diversified. In such case, the designer should unify the color and choose matching secondary color to enhance the atmosphere. The dominant color generally contrasts with the secondary color in terms of light and shade, as well as warmth and coldness. But the exact matching scheme is based on the designer's personal preference and what the illustration is finally used for.

Adjust the composition and add elements such as ceiling and roof windows to enhance credibility

Work on the colors, and manage the changes and matching of color

❺ Add Elements and Elaborate on Details

The designer has added the secondary lighting sources. Though this illustration is titled as "The Lattern Street," I don't want to put too many lighting sources in case that intricate webs of lighting will disturb the light and shade effects in the afternoon. Therefore, I have installed four lanterns on the street side to adoren the street, diversify the color palette and highlight the theme. Two ribbons of translucent crimson silk suspend from the ceiling, bringing diversity to the regular structure of the roof window as well as enhancing the atmosphere and color effects. What should be noted is that the designer should take consideration of changes to light and shade effects after adding large-scale elements illuminated by the major lighting source.

Add the major objects

The designer is supposed to elaborate on the details while keeping the major objects in mind. In this case, the major objects are obviously the first store which is the closest to the viewer's eyes.

While elaborating on the illustration, the designer is supposed to ensure that details and structure of every element has to accord with the overall atmosphere. The color added should add radiance to the dominant hue.

Elaborate on the details

By spending more effort on the details of the major objects in the foreground and less effort on the objects in the background, the sense of space and depth of field have been created, the distance between different objects in the illustration having been seemingly enlarged.

Then, the designer has added the bank lights to enhance the atmosphere. Just like the crimson silk which functions to add radiance to the dominant lanterns, the bank lights match with these lanterns in color, lighting effects and atmosphere. The reason to choose bank lights is that they can highlight the sense of clamor without producing chaos or jeopardizing the major lighting effects.

Elaborate by focusing on the theme and distinguishing between dominant and secondary elements

Eventually, the designer has added the glow and smoke to enhance the atmosphere. In this way, an ancient street with spots of lantern lights in the afternoon has been vividly depicted.

There is a little difference between the finish and the original concept. Readers could go further to experiment with different expressive approaches depending on his personal intentions and preferential style.

Add atmosphere elements such as the glow and smoke, and make the corresponding adjustments before the illustration is finished

b. *The Triumphant Return*

We will take *The Triumphant Return* as an example to illustrate how to create wide-angle environment illustrations.

❶ Concept Development

The illustration named *The Triumphant Return* depicts a scene in ancient China. People are screaming with joy when saluting the generals and soldiers who have just returned from a victorious battle. In order to avoid depicting the crowds in a painstaking way, the point of sight has been positioned in the corridor bordering the palace. A wide-angle perspective has been used to give a paronamic view of the palace and a close shot of the elegance of the interior, creating a diversity of sceneries and enhancing the sense of depth in the illustration.

❷ Composition

The designer has worked on the drafts based on his design concept, just like in the former case. The designer is also supposed to pay attention to the credibility of the persepctive and lighting effects. Different objects in this illustration face different directions. Positioned in varied ways, the objects are overlapping with each other. In this case, the designer is expected to consider how to assign every object to an optimal place. The perspective relationships between objects should be uniform. The screening object should be put where it belongs, without affecting the objects at the back.

Draft

Perspective

❸ Color Management

The illustration is intended to exude a sense of contaminating excitement. The awe-striking imperial palace should brim over with the exciting atmosphere. Therefore, the dominant hue in the illustration belongs to warm colors, contrasting with the small amount of cold color deliberately applied in the darkness and the sky.

❹ Adding Significant Elements

The stateliness of the Imperial Palace has been highlighted by the soldiers stationed at the front of the contruction. The stiffened backs of the soldiers are easy to depict, and give a sense of solemnity. Besides, by introducing these figures, the otherwise ordinary scene design illustration is bustling with vigor and vividness. The crimson silk and lanterns suspended from the roof exemplify the sense of excitement. The crowds at the foot of the palace are wild with excitement. The drifting crimson silk obscured the cradle lights inside the palace, brimming over with a sense of mystery.

Color management

Add significant elements

❺ Elaborate on the Details

This scene design illustration is more complicated than the former case. Therefore, the designer is supposed to take more consideration when working on the details. In this case, the designer should stick to the rule to focus on the close-shot objects and spend less and less effort on the receding long-shot objects. As there is a rich variety of objects in the illustration, all the objects should radiate from the point of sight, no matter it belongs to the horizontal or the vertical.

The walls closest to viewers' eyes are seen as "Line 1." In this sense, the pillars at a larger distance is seen as "Line 2," with the troops as "Line 3." When working on the details, the designer is supposed to spend less and less effort moving from Line 1 to Line 3. As to the objects in each line, the designer is expected to observe the rule of making the objects nearby detailed and those afar simple. For example, the soldier closest to the viewers' eyes should be depicted in a careful way, while those faraway should be roughly drawn. This rule also applies to other objects such as lanterns and silks.

Elaborate on the illustration

Work on the details

❻ Enhance Atmosphere

Atmosphere is a highlight in this illustration. The designer has illustrated the flowers and ribbons drifting in the air in celebration of the rejoicing crowds, highlighting the atmosphere of excitement projected by troops on their return from a victorious battle and crowds warmly welcoming their heroes. Some pedals could drift into the construction where the point of sight has been positioned. In adding the atmosphere elements, the designer also has to consider the presepective relationship and scenery composition. In addition, he should take good account of the credibility for what atmosphere elements should be incorporated in the illustration and how these elements should be presented. For example, the wind direction and wind force should have an identical effect on the ribbons, banners, and lanterns. (We will talk more about atmosphere enhancement in the later chapters.)

Enhance atmosphere

Summary

If we counpare landscape illustrations to historical legends, then the environment illustrations could be compared to verse and prose. Though the latter category cannot impress the viewers with a sense of magnificence, it is able to touch the viewers emotionally. The designer can use environment illustrations to create a rich variety of atmosphere and impressions.

In dealing with this category of illustrations, the designer should think of incorporating certain plots instead of approaching it as an ordinary scene. Even though it is likely that there is no figure in the illustration, every element should be special in a certain way that interweaves with each other to tell a story.

Environment illustrations are commonly used in scene design. It is highly recognizable, and powerfully impressive. When working on this category of illustrations, the designer should notice that in addition to techniques and concept, visual effects and impact, color matching, as well as atmosphere enhancement are all essential factors to environment illustrations. All these factors can help to make the illustrations more visually appealing, elevating the illustrations to a higher level.

Gallery

Forest

Software: Painter

The designer has given prominence to the drifting mist shrouding the forest, and the hundreds of birds flapping their wings in the sky, incorporating dynamics with tranquility and enhancing the vividness. This composition approach has fully demonstrated how to match the medium-shot objects with each other.

The Bridge

Software: Painter

In the illustration, the ancient stone bridge is bathed in the morning light. Coupled with lighting effects and atmosphere effects, the gradation in the medium-shot and long-shot objects has become distinctive by prioritizing the objects nearby and handling with the objects afar in a rough way.

Relics

Software: Painter

A temple is nestled in thick forests. Weathered for centuries, the temple has already lost its original glory and become decayed. This illustration has referred to the Angkor Wat, while incorporating the designer's wisdom. The approaches of environment illustrations applies espeeially to depictions of the

Morning

Software: Painter

In the morning, the sunshine illuminates a virtual city. In order to better illustrate the morning sunshine, the designer has given a transparent effect to many constructions.

The Village

Software: Painter

The warm-color ed sunshine glows on the constructions in the village. The designer has started with the objects on the ground and moved to those afar to create an overarching atmosphere of tranquility and harmony.

The Chapel

Software: Painter

Depicting an interior scene, the designer has focused on the close-shot and medium-shot objects due to spatial restriction. This illustration has broadened the visual range with a distorted perspective (a perspective other than fisheye-view wide angle) to give full expression to the holiness of the chapel.

C. Urban Architecture

Overview

Gallery

C. Urban Architecture

Overview

Urban architecture can be presented by using either landscape illustrations or environment illustrations. We have selected an independent section to talk about urban architecture not only because it is a very distinctive subject, but also that architecture occupies a dominant place in scene design works, making it necessary to clearly explain the complex perspective and structural relationship. How to capture the unique features of the urban architecture and employ 3D software to illustrate the architecture constitute a significant topic to discuss about in this section.

In addition to structure and perspective, depiction of lighting texture is indispensable for such works. No matter it is a fantasy city or an ancient town, towering building or narrow streets, any kind of architecture should feature a realistic style. Although it is not necessary that the architecture looks like those in the real life, it must possesses a sense of existence. As the architecture stands right in front of the viewers, it should not be associated with virtual elements. Even in a distorted and eerie space, the architecture should be configured as something of a considerable scale and solid texture.

As viewers of illustrations are mostly based in the city, they will feel more familiar with scene design works on urban architecture than other categories. Thus, urban architecture has become a favorite both for scene designers and for the advertising agents.

I. Concept Development

Urban architecture illustrations are different from other categories only in terms of subject and techniques. Therefore, it is a common choice for landscape illustrations and environment illustrations. In the initial stage, the designer should determine the overall atmosphere, no matter it is a sense of vastness or crowdedness. Then, the designer should decide on the top priority and the ambience of this illustration. The last step before sketching is to search for referential materials following the specific reguirements.

Some referential photos that depict urban architecture

II. Basic Composition and Drafts

Urban architecture illustrations feature a considerable number of objects which are placed in a regular and diversified way, creating complex perspectives and structures. But how can a designer make sure that the prioritization status for each object is appropriate with a clear sense of gradation? This is a guestion the designer should bear in mind right from the initial drafting and composition phases.

a. Composition in Landscape Illustrations

In landscape illustrations, urban architecture is often depicted by using a bird's-eye view to encompass more objects. Readers can refer to the gallery part in the first section of this chapter.

Aside from employing the bird's-eye view, the designer can also position the viewers' sight in the skycraper, as if they are looking down from the window. This approach is different from a simple bird's-eye view considering that gradation in the illustrations has been diversified by incorporating close-shot and interior elements.

Architectural complex in a wide-angle landscape illustration

The sense of depth and gradation effects in this outdoor scene featuring wide angle and long shot is enhanced by incorporating the medium-shot and close-shot interior elements.

As the overlapping between the buildings have blocked the sight, neither a horizontal view nor slightly worm's-eye view can illustrate a scene featuring magnificence and vastness. The aforementioned perspectives are only suitable for the spacious area such as the center of the square in the city. In this case, the surrounding objects should be manipulated in such a way so as to enhance the wide-angle effects, enabling the viewers to feel like looking around in the very center. In some occasions, the "fisheye view" perspective can be employed to make the illustration more visually striking.

b. Composition in the Environment Illustrations

In environment illustrations, urban architecture is usually approached as observed by ordinary people. In this case, only what an ordinary person can see will be selected in the illustration. This approach brings a breath of familiarity to the viewers, even though the work itself might deal with fantastical or futuristic topics.

A narrow street depicted in an environment illustration

An example of interiors in a given architecture

Different perspectives apply to different occassions. For example, when illustrating an awe-inspiring architecture or architectural complex, it is advised to position the viewer's eye on the ground to look up, which will highlight a sense of magnificence or oppression. A horizontal view at the ground level will help to demonstrate the rich details of medium-shot or close-shot objects or the gradation relationship between some long-shot objects and close-shot objects, giving prominence to the sense of prosperity and depth. All these perspectives also apply to presenting varied interior effects of different kinds of architecture.

A second example of interiors in a given architecture

III. Techniques for Urban Architecture

Based on what tools to use, we can roughly divide urban architecture illustrations into four categories, namely traditional 2D illustration, photo-blended 2D illustration, 3D illustration, and 2D illustration processed with 3D software.

When working on urban architecture topics, it is very important to select optimal illustration approaches, which means the designer is supposed to select the one that most fits his works. As the structure, perspective as well as light and shade effects are very complicated in such illustrations, the designer has to keep in mind the mutual impacts between varied objects while considering other basic factors such as objects, atmosphere, details and theme. As scene illustrations on urban architecture are closer to daily lilfe, it will be relatively easy for the viewers to spot any flaw in the illustrations, which will definitely affect the overall coherence of a given work. In such a case, the traditional 2D illustrations will fail the expectations. In response to the complicated structures and perspectives, some 2D designers will choose to refer to some scenery or architecture photos featuring similar perspectives when elaborating on their illustrations. This solution does help to effectively reduce the workload involved to achieve credibility of perspective and structure in the initial or medium phase of the creative process. However, since the light and shade effects, composition, style and confguration of the referential photos are predetermined, no matter how a given photo seems to match, the finish will be considerably different from what the designer has expected in the initial stage. Thus, the designer will feel restricted in the later process, unable to unbridle his imagination and bring his skills into full play. Besides, the designer also has to spend much time in integrating the structure and lighting effects.

Different Categories of Illustrations	Softwares and Tools Used	Appropriateness for Urban Architecture	Reasons
Traditional 2D illustrations	Painter, Photoshop	★☆☆☆	The designer needs to spend much time in the composing process. There will be perspective problems if the object's structure is too complicated or if there are too many objects to draw.
photo-blended 2D illustrations	Painter, Photoshop	★★☆☆	Using these software can basically address the perspective issues, but the structure and lighting effects may be restricted by the photo.
3D illustrations	Maya, 3DS MAX	★★★☆	This solves the problems concerning perspective, structure as well as light and shade, and eliminates the limitations of photo references. However, it will take a long time, especially in the process to capture the atmosphere and details.
2D illustration processed with 3D software	Maya, 3DS MAX + Painter, Photoshop	★★★★	It is easy to achieve a relatively precise perspective, structure and lighting effect by using 3D software. Then 2D software may facilitate a quick finish to atmosphere and details.

Examples of traditional 2D illustrations

Examples of illustrations using photos as referential
background while incorporating 2D drawing techniques

Examples of 3D illustrations

As a matter of fact, a considerable number of 2D illustrators only care about a relatively precise perspective, structure and lighting effect when working on this category of illustrations, and this could be easily achieved by using 3D software. With the advance of 3D software, more and more well-performing 3D software that are easier to learn to operate have come to be accepted by 2D artists as a common tool for 2D architecture illustrations, while some artists good at managing 3D scenery have even switched to 3D illustration. They have made impressive performance in this field by taking full advantage of their experience and techniques in traditional 2D illustration while utilizing 3D software featuring high level of precision and striking expressive powers.

In addition, what is noteworthy is that illustrators will come up with varied effects and have various considerations when using different illustration tools. In the illustrations highlighting 3D effects, how to enhance the atmosphere and depict the details is a top concern — 3D software boasts outstanding performance in terms of lighting effects and sense of space, and therefore there's no need to worry about the precision of the structure and perspective. On the other hand, in illustrations celebrating 2D effects, the artist relies almost completely on band-drawing kills without the assistance of computer calculation. Then, how to approach the overall atmosphere as well as perspective, structure and lighting effect should be prioritized.

Both 2D and 3D illustrations have their distinctive advantages. An artist cannot succeed without calculated application and full exploitation of the advantages of either category.

Refer to the configuration, perspective, proportion, positioning and lighting effects in the 3D model for 2D illustrations

IV. Case Studies

Many professional 2D artists are eager to use 3D software to avoid disadvantages of 2D software in terms of spatial structure. However, most 3D software elevate their works to a higher level, no matter how human-oriented, is impossible to grasp even for the most brilliant beginners without insightful instruction or helpful textbooks. At present, most tutorial materials on 3D software in the market are too complicated for having listed all the functions of certain software one by one, most of which are meaningless to 2D artists. As they cannot access the auxiliary functions of the software in a straightforward way, many have given up their attempts, which is really a pity. In the following passages, I will exemplify how to apply the basic functions of 3D software to create 3D architecture illustrations in the easiest and quickest way, which, I hope, could bing inspirations to the readers in certain ways.

a. *Ancient Street*

Take *Ancient Street* for example, I'll demonstrate how to utilize 3D software to draw urban architecture illustrations.

❶ Concept Development

The illustration features an integration of traditional Chinese-style architecture and Tibetan construction — moist pavement, towering walls and long street all indicate a sense of mystery. This illustration has selected a typical mode for environment illustrations, and an identical angle of view with *Lattern Street,* the work discussed earlier in this chapter. Moreover, this illustration also applies a common eye-level view to demonstrate the sense of depth. This example will show that illustrations featuring the same category and angle of view may be concerned with different effects and different procedures due to the different platforms to be employed.

With the rapid development in the CG industry, most 3D software has come closer and closer to perfection through constant updates. Well-developed software such as 3DS MAX, MAYA, Softimage have made enormous contributions to the film, advertising, and game industries, while making a more and more active presence in our daily life. Due to their human-oriented operation platforms and outstanding competence, they have become the favorites of 3D lovers and CG artists. All these softwares perform well when it comes to uncomplicated model making, light rendering and texture editing. They basically share common operation rules and differ from each other merely in terms of menu and interface. Therefore, those interested in this field can rely on their own preferences to select adequate software for learning or creative purposes.

Considering the convenience factor, I will use 3DS MAX in the following example, which is easier for beginners. All the following effects and procedures can apply to other softwares. What is supposed to be demonstrated here highlights the creative process and personal experience in the making of 3D illustrations, which could be shared by all the 3D softwares.

"Ancient Street"

❷ Modeling

In 3DS MAX, "BOX" is used as the standard primitive to emulate the objects in the scene. The illustrator is expected to start from the ground and gradually move upwards to the architecture, followed by adjusting the proportional relationship and placing the objects where they belong. In order to achieve a relatively uniform effect, a grey material is applied to all the models (as the number 1 indicates in the picture on the right). Models of different heights have formed two rows, leaving the middle opening as the street itself. The blue camera icon marks out where the point of view is supposed to be.

A virtual 3D space has taken the place of the traditional 2D plane in the making of 3D scenery. Unlike in 2D illustrations where the artist draws drafts and elaborates on it later based on the predetermined angle of view, the artist has to deal with the 3D objects in the picture one after another in a realistic way. Though seemingly complicated, 3D illustrations generally cost less time than the traditional 2D category because this realistic approach ensures that the perspective and structure of the illustration are precise and flawless. In addition, a well-constructed scenery can be approached from any angle of view, like using a camera to take a picture from any position in the real world. Therefore, the designer can change the angle of view due to special requirements and select an optimal position for presentation, which demonstrates another advantage of 3D illustrations over their 2D counterparts.

❸ Setting up the Lighting Source

A pair of "Omni" has been set up in the upper part — one is placed higher to emulate the sunshine (the dominant lighting source), while the other is positioned above the end of the street, which will be used to emulate the misty effect later (as indicated by the number 2 in the picture on the right). In addition, a "skylight" has been set up to bathe the scenery in daylight after rendering. As this command applies to the entire scene, the icon can be randomly placed (as indicated by the number 2 in the lower-right corner of the picture on the right). Choose "Mental Ray" and tick "Enable" under "Final Gather," and click the "Render" button at the bottom of the "Render Scene" menu. The illustration will then demonstrate the overall lighting effect (as indicated by the number 3 in the picture on the right).

Switch the point of view to the predetermined position of "camera," and the initial effect of the street will be right before our eyes. The designer can make further adjustments to the heights and positions of the constructions for an optimal effect.

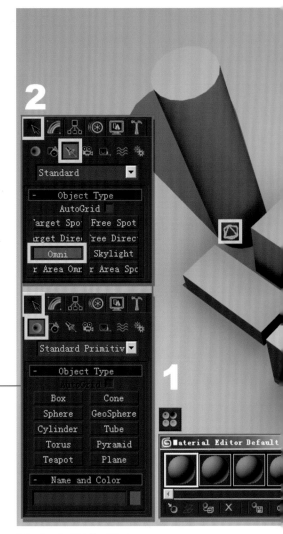

Adjusting the Lighting Effect

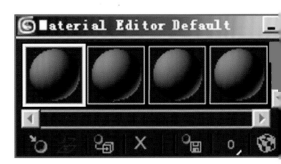

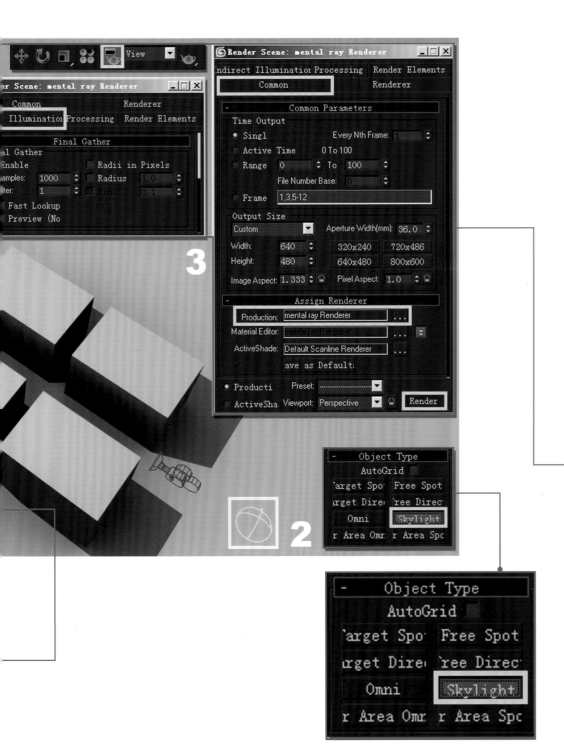

3

2

Render Scene: mental ray Renderer

Common | Renderer
Indirect Illumination Processing | Render Elements

Common Parameters

Time Output
- Single   Every Nth Frame: 1
- Active Time   0 To 100
- Range   0   To   100
  File Number Base: 0
- Frame   1,3,5-12

Output Size
Custom   Aperture Width(mm): 36.0
Width: 640   320x240   720x486
Height: 480   640x480   800x600
Image Aspect: 1.333   Pixel Aspect: 1.0

Assign Renderer
Production: mental ray Renderer   ...
Material Editor: mental ray Renderer   ...
ActiveShade: Default Scanline Renderer   ...
ave as Default:
- Producti   Preset: ------------
- ActiveSha   Viewport: Perspective   Render

Object Type
AutoGrid
Target Spo   Free Spot
rget Dire   ree Direc
Omni   **Skylight**
r Area Omr   r Area Spc

❹ Adjusting the Lighting Effect

Select the "Omni" at the highest point (the dominant lighting source mentioned befove), and make adjustments by clicking "Modify." Tick "On" for "Shadows" in the "General Parameters" menu, and select "Ray Traced Shadow" to cast shadows. In order to highlight the contrast between light and shadow in the scene, the light should be moved to the left, leaving one side of the street well-illuminated and the other side poorly-illuminated to make the illustration more visually appealing. As the emulated sunshine is highly illuminating, the parameter in "Multiplier" in the "Intensity/ Color/ Attenuation" menu should be raised to 3. If the rendered effect suffers from over exposure, the designer should adopt a similar procedure by selecting "Skylight" and make adjustments on "Modify", reducing the "Multiplier" to around 0.3.

❺ Emulating the Misty Effect

Select the "Omni" above the street end to emulate the misty effect, and click "Modify" pane 1 to make adjustments. As this "Omni" is intended to create the misty effect rather than to illuminate, "On" should not be clicked for "Shadows." Instead, the designer is supposed to initiate the "Volume Light" in the "Atmospheres & Effects" menu to emulate a misty weather. At this time, "Multiplier" should be set at 0.3 to illustrate the misty effect, while how far the "mist" creeps should be changed by managing "Omni" with zoom tools. All these effects cannot be seen until rendered. Therefore, a satisfactory effect is a product of repetitive tests and adjustments of the parameters.

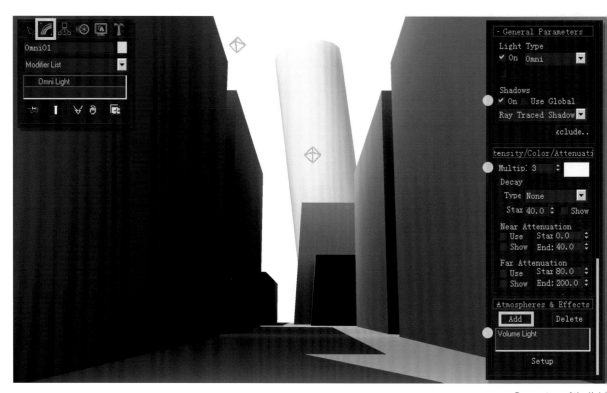

Parameters of the light

Enhance the "Volume Light" to emulate the misty effect

➏ Creating 2D Illustrations After Modeling

At this time, 2D artists can start to draw 2D illustrations on the basis of the 3D model. A correct lighting effect, balanced spatial relationship between objects, suitable positioning of angle of view and composition, along with a precise perspective and sense of space, all of these important factors to architecture illustrations. Basic knowledge concerning the application of 3D software as mentioned above can satisfy the general requirements of those illustrators majoring in 2D illustrations. In order to make it easier to understand, only simple examples are used here. The artists can base on their personal requirements to construct complicated 3D scenes by using various standard primitives.

The picture in the lower right corner was the 2D architecture illustration created on the basis of the relatively complicated 3D scene modeled after this approach. Drawing 2D illustrations has become much easier thanks to the precise structure and perspective — the designer no longer needs to take much consideration of relevant apsects, which has helped to quicken the drawing process.

An experienced 2D scene designer can create equally impressive illustrations by solely depending on the traditional approach as well. However, it is certain that he has to spend much more time and effort, which can be avoided in the 3D approach. In addition to this merit, using 3D software can ensure continuity between blueprints and design sketches as well as coherence in terms of proportion and structure. In 3D scenes, the designer can adjust the viewpoint in an unrestrained way, making it easy to produce three-view drawings and drawings featuring varied perspectives for reference.

2D scene illustration created
by referring to the 3D model

❼ Elaborating on the 3D model

We have talked about how to draw 2D scene illustrations by using 3D reference drawings. At this stage, the artists who have intended to solely depend on the 3D approach when working on this category of illustrations have to further elaborate the model.

In this process, every "BOX" or any other standard primitive used to emulate the scene is seen as a "target object." We need to replace it with 3D models of equal proportion and high precision. High-precision models are developed based on the original concept. One way is to continue to add details to the existing model; or we can transform the standard primitives into "Editable Poly" or "Editable Mesh," and use various commands in "Modify" for the editing purpose. All these methods are explained in a meticulous way in any reference book on 3D software. Thus, we will save the energy to elaborate on them one by one. The artists interested in this field can go further to make bold experiments and attempts to create their own 3D world.

❽ Drawing, Applying and Rendering Texture Mapping

At last, the designer has to construct the UV Map and apply texture mapping. Texture mapping refers to the patterns applied on the model's surface to represent different colors, motif, texture and other detailed effects, while UV is the coordinate setting of the patterns in the model. Other reference books also touch upon these theories and the exact process in a detailed way. I will only focus on texture mapping in the following passages, which is a determinant to the artistic quality of the finish.

Add details to the model

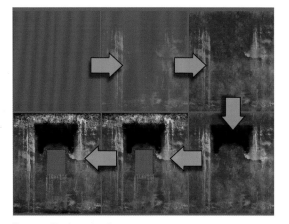

Process of texture mapping

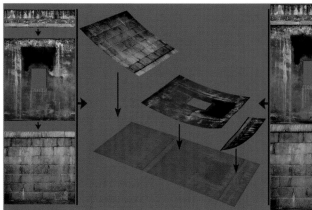

Process to make complicated textures through patching

Texture diversification

We can use Photoshop's "Overlay" function to draw the mapping for the walls of Tibetan temples, and apply stone-texture materials to highlight that the originally crimson walls that have already been weathered.

When working on the mapping, the designer should consider whether the corresponding effects will match the environment, which will finally determine whether the finish looks real. Take this illustration for example. After centuries, the walls originally coated with red mineral paints should be dotted with stains left by the rain, and the surface should start to fall off. Therefore, the designer has to think about the theme and subject in a cautious way when working on every illustration. Delicate details are not always wanted.

The designer should finish constructing the texture on the foundation and top layer in the same way and combine them together afterwards. Regular mapping will make it easier to observe the effects in a straightforward way. Composite as a product of various mappings combined together should be uniform in texture and precision degree.

Due to centuries of weathering effects, every part of the construction should be damaged to a certain extent. In order to make it realistic, the designer has to make overall adjustments and transfer one set of mapping into multiple sets by using Photoshop's "Stamp" tool.

After applying the mapping to all the objects, the designer should start rendering and adjusting. It should be noted that extra light and shadow should be avoided for the mapping, since in 3D scenes, all the lighting effects are justified as results of redering calculations. Thus, the designer needs to select illustrations of zero diopter.

The creation of *Ancient Street* is finally finished after elaborating, mapping, adjusting the lighting effects and other processes.

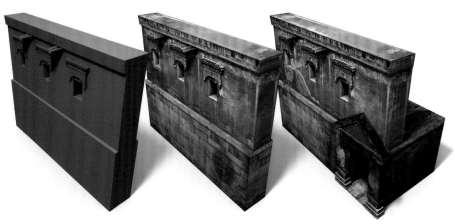

Final effects of texture mapping on the model

Adjust various parameters to achieve a desired finished.

b. *Red Trolley Bus*

I will take *Red Trolley Bus* as an example to explain how to create relatively complicated 3D urban architecture illustrations and share with the readers some of my personal experience.

❶ Concept Development

The designer has selected red as the dominant hue and the cold tones in the sky as a secondary role. This illustration depicts an afternoon on a tranquil antique street that nestled among towering skyscrapers in a rustling city. There is no vehicle or crowd except for a crawling red trolley bus. A sense of warmth and tranquility poses sharp contrast to the coldness of the city.

In this illustration, a traditional viewpoint is used to depict the urban architecture. However, unlike *Ancient Street*, the viewpoint has been shifted downwards to the right, with an enlarged vision featuring wide angle and a slightly-elevated perspective. Therefore, the trolley bus as the major object runs directly to the audience, leaving enough room to exhibit the cityscape, making the illustration more visually appealing. Towering skyscrapers and the ancient street have formed up a ragged outline. Such a compact structure has a positive effect on the overall color variation.

"Red Trolley Bus"

Set up models, adjust the lighting effect for the rendering process

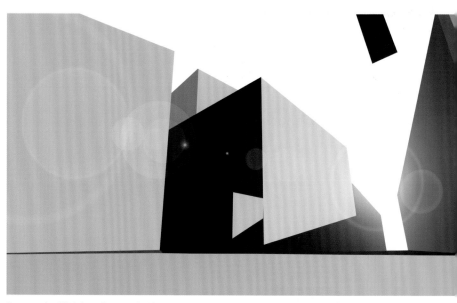

An example of lighting effects and white-and-black grid

Effects after the texture mapping is applied.

❷ Setting up models and lighting source

Set up the model in the same way as mentioned above and test the lighting effect. The designer has to take more considerations when testing the lighting effect because the scene has become more complicated. The pictures above show the final choice of the lighting effect after comparing different rendering effects by placing primary lighting source in different locations.

The illustration is generally well-illuminated, as the timing is set for the afternoon. Sunshine finds its way from between the buildings, leaving a contrast of light and shade, just like an intricate chessboard.

❸ Adding Texture Mapping and Rendering

After adding texture mapping to major objects such as buildings, trolley bus and the ground, it's fime for the rendering process, and the overall look of this old street has been thus determined.

Add the environmental elements including the blue sky and cold-tone skyscrapers. In order to facilitate a perfect integration of the background and foreground, the designer should reduce the saturation of red mapping for the old street, and change the "Volume Light" in "Omni" into light blue so that the end of the street will melt into the blue sky.

At last, the designer should add the glow and smoke to enhance the atmosphere. At this stage, *Red Trolley Bus* is finished.

Add long-shot scenery

Summary

Case studies in this chapter demonstrates a few fundamental and beginner-friendly creative approaches integrating both 2D and 3D software. They are intended to stir some traditional 2D artists' interests in 3D creation. In addition to popularizing the basic procedure in 3D creation, it is intended to demonstrate the diversification of creative approaches. Both 2D and 3D software are merely creative tools for artists. Only by utilizing these tools in an optimal way can an artist create illustrations of vitality. In contrast to traditional artistic forms, CG arts and illustration art are considerably new. The themes and creative approaches they are concerned with are more innovative and diversified. Artists engaged in this area should perfect themselves by grasping more tools to enhance their powers of expression. 3D softwares perform well on urban architecture illustrations because this catagory features high requirements in spatial relationship and structure. 2D artists earnest to make attempts in 3D creation are advised to start with urban architecture first. In the later chapters, more illustrations using 3D software will be exhibited, which is intended to facilitate a comprehensive understanding of this field on the part of artists who know little about 3D creation.

Enhance atmosphere by adding glow and smoke. The illustration is finished.

Gallery

Pagoda

Software: 3DS MAX

Thick wires extend from the small
town to the towering pagoda in
the distance. The entire picture is
shrouded in a death-like tranquility.

Babylon

Three Kingdoms — Interior

Software: 3DS MAX

This set of illustrations depicts architectural interiors in Three Kingdoms Period of Chinese history. All the works feature a uniform style as they are to be used in the same computer game. 3D software have been used to set up models to ensure a precise perspective and lighting effect, and facilitate a uniformity in color, texture and style so that all the illustrations will seem to belong to the same set.

The Gate

Software: 3DS MAX

This illustration is also intended to exemplify the overall lighting effect. The composition is intended to highlight the sense of depth of the street.

D. Atmosphere

Overview

Gallery

D. Atmosphere

Overview

In the previous seetions, we have discussed scene design issues including themes, materials, ways of presentation and approaches. I've also emphasized on the impotant aspects sach as composition, perspective and the use of 2D / 3D softwares. In addition, all the categories of scene design illustrations are concerned with an integral element, atmosphere. Though indispensable, atmosphere is very likely to be neglected. It is neither a real object nor a special presentation approach. It has something to do with moods or feelings. Good atmosphere will trigger certain emotions on the part of the audience, making it easier to comprehend the theme of the illustration and to capture the defining features of the scenery.

A scene illustration without an adequate atmosphere is like a man without any personality, which will obscure the theme embedded, making it difficult to excite and engage the audience. On contrary, a scene illustration with a matching atmosphere would become something with soul, personality and life, evolving into a work of art. In this sense, an illustration without theme or atmosphere is just a landscape photo that lacks vitality and soul.

"Buildings in the Mist" is a scene illustration with powerful atmosphere.

I. Categorization of Atmosphere

Generally speaking, atmosphere is intended to accentuate on a certain theme or suggest certain moods. Though atmosphere is all about the subjective impressions of the audience, it might either focus on what natural scene looks like or how people feel about something. In the former case, natural phenomena such as chill or heat are highlighted, while in the latter case, sentimental elements are exploited, including grief, joy and so on. Atmosphere themed on natural environments is supposed to observe scientific laws, and the designer is only concerned about how to make real scenery more beautiful. With regards to the other category, the designer will need to take more considerations and be emotionally involved in the creative process.

An illustration with an atmosphere focused on natural phenomena

An illustration with an atmosphere targeted at the emotional response

What does a designer need to do to make a scene design illustration emotionally provocative without the help of characters? Generally speaking, how a scene illustration will impress the audience in an emotional way is mostly determined by how the designer feels when working on it. Actually, this rule does not only apply to this specific category. All creative illustrations are based on inspirations, while inspirations are a product of human sensual experience. When working on commissions, a scene designer might feel himself restrained because the illustrations have to be commercially functional in the first place. However, even in this case, an artist would still infuse personal emotions and moods into the illustration. Such emotions or moods could be exploited and magnified in the works to enhance the atmosphere.

II. Elements to Capture the Atmosphere

In most cases, a designer should encapsulate the defining features of natural phenomena from a scientific perspective, and then try to amplify those details that are commonly neglected in an artistic way. For example, a gust of wind could be indicated through a maze of leaves tossed around in the air, the scorching weather may be suggested by distorting the scenery in the distance, and the commotion can be expressed by obscuring the motions of the surrounding objects.

A scene designer can also depend on some natural elements when working on emotionally provocative illustrations. In this case, it's important to choose some special environments to illustrate a particular atmosphere, taking advantage of the empathy effects to trigger certain sentimental responses.

Elements	Cases to Capture Cetain Moods
Climate	People will feel depressed when dark clouds screen the sunshine, and feel rejoiced at the sight of glittering sunshine and the white clouds contrasting the crystal blue sky.
Space	A stuffed room will make people feel like choking, while a spacious hall can make people breathe easy.
Different hours of a day, and the four seasons	Twilights make people feel grieved; the tranquil night has a calming effect; the refreshing chill in the morning engenders hopes, while a muggy summer afternoon is boring. Spring stands for vitality, summer for vibrancy, autumn for gloom while winter for silence.
Special Scenery	Decayed ruins make people feel sad, while congested streets make them edgy.
Color	Warm tones generate a sense of warmth, while cold tones are associated with tranquility and stillness.
Lights	A dimly-lit room is fear-striking, while a well-illuminated environment will make people feel at ease.

Twilights exude a sense of gloominess

III. Case Studies

a. *Dance of Wind*

We will take *Dance of Wind* for example to illustrate how to enhance atmosphere through depiction of natural environment.

❶ Concept Development

Wind is invisble. In this illustration, I have chosen to depict the drifting flowers which have dotted the ancient pagoda and stone bridge to make the audience feel the movement of the wind. Due to their tiny size, I have selected blue as the dominant tone for the rest of the scenery to contrast with the pink petals. Millions of flower petals flow with wind, as if joyfully dancing in the air. I have depended on the movements of the falling flowers to capture the motions of the wind, so as to give prominence to the theme and highlight the atmosphere by incorporating both the static and the dynamic.

"Dance of Wind"

❷ Drafting

This illustration is intended to depict how elegantly the flowers dance in the wind. Out of consideration of the atmosphere, other major objects should be obscured. Therefore, there objects are positioned on the periphery, and a worm's eye-view has been adopted to reveal an expansive sky, which serves as the foil to the core objects — the flowers. The bridge is diagonally placed. I have utilized the "atmosphere effect" on the bridge, making it melt into the background to put a distance between the audience and the bridge so that it will not steal thunder from the petals in the foreground. Besides, I have added mountains between the bridge and the sky to enhance a sense of depth.

❸ Working on the Initial Draft

This stage is concerned with elaborating on the objects in focus by illustrating their texture and composition. It is advised to start with objects that are closer to the viewpoint and move further and further away, spending more time on the dominant objects while dealing with the insignificant elements in a rough way. A designer should be concerned about color matching the seguence of the objects. I have painted the branches and leaves of the peach tree on the right in a meticulous way and those on the left and in the lower part in a rough way so as to create a sense of depth.

❹ How to Capture the Falling Flowers

To make it realistic, I have assigned three layers when working on the falling flowers so that it looks as if some are closer to the audience than others (I have temporarily chosen black as background to make it easier to understand). The first layer is given to the close-up objects, which is nearer to the audience than all the other objects. Due to the perspective effect, they will appear larger and lustrous However, it should be noted that the flowers should not be over-amplified in size to the extent of disproportion. The next is the medium-shot layer, which is essential to capture the movements of the wind. This layer is supposed to occupy a relatively spacious section. The petals on this layer should appear smaller and translucent in order to distinguish from those in the

The initial draft

Elaborate on the details

Flowers drifting in the air

A falling flower, a core object, contrasts with the flying petals in the background, creating a view featuring impressive dynamics.

foreground. What comes last is the long-shot layer. The petals on this layer feature a lighter hue, scattered everywhere in order to make a difference to the regularity in the former layers, constructing an integral and natural wholeness. At last, I have blurred the petals based on their movements and obscured them to enhance the sense of motion in the illustration.

Flying petals have been added to the illustration. The movements of the winds have become visible to the audience through the drifting petals, which have breathed life and soul into an otherwise tranquil scene.

Add glow to the combined scene, and make an overall adjustment. This scene illustration which is intended to highlight the environmental atmosphere is finally finished.

b. *Tree of Happiness*

In the following passages, I will take *Tree of Happiness* as an example to talk about how to address the emotional experience of the audience in scene illustrations. I have chosen 3D software throughout the production process to make clear the difference in 2D and 3D illustrations concerning atmosphere enhancement.

❶ Concept Development

The illustration is aimed at giving expression to a joyful and high-spirited mood. Based on this predetermined theme, I have decided to capture such a scene: at dawn, the breeze has sucked away the mist which has enveloped the valley. A glittering star sweeps across the sky and pitched down. At the same time, beams of light shoot up, illuminating the red branches and leaves of an ancient tree as if in daylight. The inspirations for this illustration come from a giant Christmas tree standing on the square at Christmas time. Its branches interwine with millions of colorful lights, and the entire square overflows with joy. During the process to relive that happy moment, I have added to this illustration some typical Oriental elements.

"Tree of Happiness"

❷ Drafts and Sketches

3D illustrations feature a higher precision standard than the 2D ones, and thus take more time to produce. Coupled with the difference in approach, the designer cannot see what the finish will look like until the last moment. When working on the realistic-style illustrations, the draft is not that important, because the designer can refer to some materials such as photos. However, as to fantasy illustrations, a designer is advised to put down all his illusions on paper in one shot in case the original concept will fade away in his memory as time goes by in the creative process. By visualizing what has inspired him in the draft, the designer can relive the atmosphere and his feelings at any time by taking a look at the draft. In order to highlight the festive joy, I have chosen red and yellow (warm tones) as the dominant hue of the illustration.

❸ How to Use the 3D Technique to Depict Details

We should start by creating a tree based image. Here, we will still depend on some basic functions of 3DS MAX software. As shown in the illustration, choose "Foliage" under "AEC Extended," which is a MAX composite tool for creating trees.

Parameters of Foliage

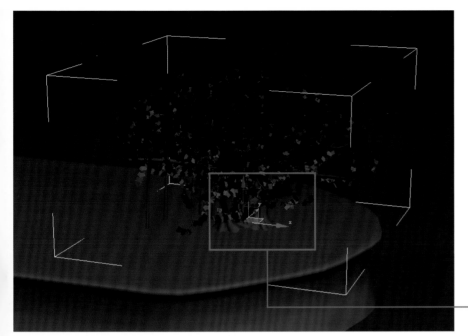

Select the "Banyan tree" which looks like the one in the draft, and set it up on the finished platform.

Use "Modify" function on the editing list and make adjustments to the tree model for the desired result. It should be noted that the designer will end up with a randomly-created tree by clicking the "New" button on the left of "Seed" under "Parameters." If it's chosen repeatedly, the designer cannot easily go back to the original state for comparison. Therefore, it is advised to use the parameters on the right of "Seed" for the adjusting purpose. Below "Show" are the component elements for the tree. The designer can delete unwanted components based on their particular requirements. For example, this illustration is concerned with a sturdy ancient tree. Though "Banyan tree" looks similar to what we want, its roots are unneeded, and should thus be deleted from the list. A designer will have to make such selections in the later process as well.

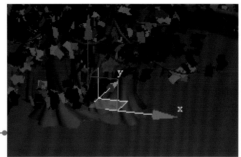

Create a tree

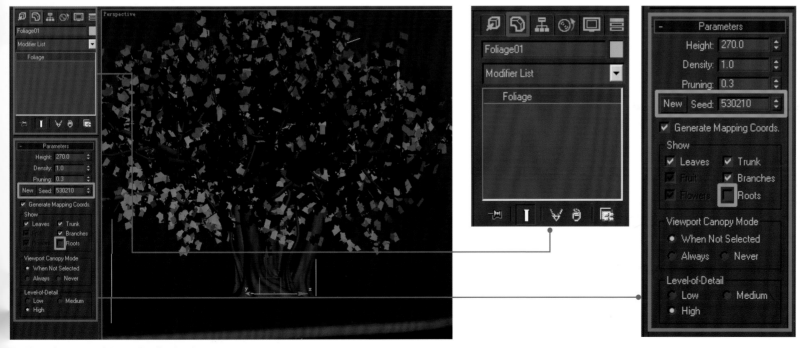

Decide on the contour of the tree by adjusting the parameters

draft. Many artistis would like to finish this process in the post-production stage. However, as this illustration is intended as a still frame with a determined composition and design concept, an easy start will save a lot of effort. For example, the designer does not have to care about the periphery outside the frame any more. Setting up the camera is aimed at locking the angle of view so that it will be easier to adjust the position and proportion of the objects.

The designer can switch to a desired angle in "Perspective" and then set up the camera based on that

locking "Free Camera" so that the angle of the camera is consistent with the "Perspective" setting. The designer can rotate "Perspective" to change the angle of view. Press "C" key, and the view will change to the "Camera," which allows the designer to observe what the finish will look like, including the positions of the objects and the final effects. Press "P" key, the view will switch to "Perspective" to make it easier to make adjustments to the model.

Fix the angle of view and set up the camera.

Click the "Material Editor" and select a new material. Use "Pick Material from Object" function to take in the texture of the "tree." You will find six materials here. Make corresponding adjustments based on the respective name of each material.

Extract the material

Start from the leaves: open up the material of the leaves, and you will find that there is a clear channel map in the default material. Click the icon of "Show Map in Viewport," and effects for leaves pruned by the channel will unfold before your eyes. Find the location of the file through the path, and extract the default map provided by MAX.

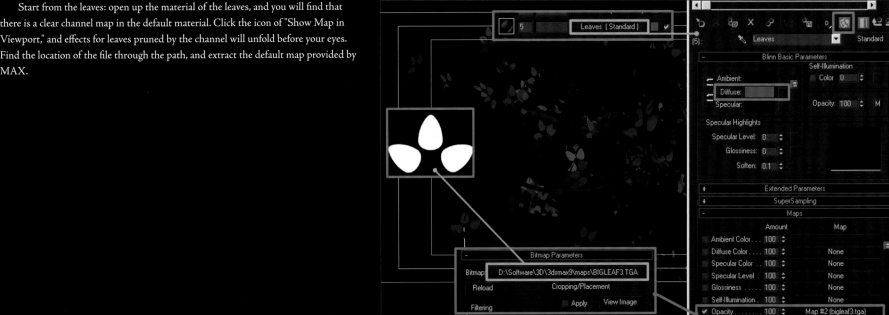

Extract the channel map of the leaves

Revise the channel map and the color of leaves for a desired effect

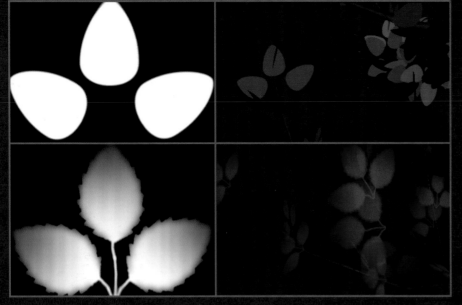

Revise the channel map of the leaves

Apply the mapping to the trunk and branches. The model is already UV-implanted. The mapping can be cycled at the will of the designer.

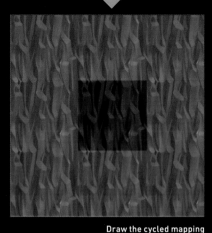

Draw the cycled mapping

Cyclic mapping refers to those which consist of identical patterns cycled and connected in four directions without seam. The designer can use the "Filter — Displace" function in Photoshop when working on such mapping.

The leaves of the "Banyan tree" are not dense enough for the finish. Thus, we can reproduce another two identical "Banyan trees," delete the trunk part and switch them to a different direction, which provides an easy remedy to this "density" problem.

Increase the density of the leave

Initial rendering

We can start to elaborate on the platform in the next stage: draw a channel map for the meadow by following the same process when working on the leaves. Paste the finished map on a patch entitled "Plane" in a cyclic way. Like the leaves, color mapping only involves color.

{ Tip }

It is advised to use jet black for the transitive purpose when drawing the outline of the channel map. Insert a black outline between the meadow and the earth to avoid sampling errors.

Draw the mapping of the meadow

Now we arrange the finished patches into a fan by following the rise and fall of the ground. When the angle of the camera approaches a horizontal view, a meadowed ground will come into existence.

Set up some rocks on the platform for diversification. Set up "Omni" as the dominant lighting source at the root, and "Skylight" as a secondary lighting source. Choose "mental ray" as the renderer and open up "Final Gather" to finish rendering.

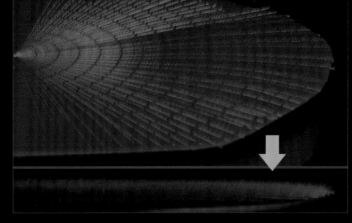

Arrange the drafting
sheets of the meadow

Set up the dominant and
secondary lighting sources

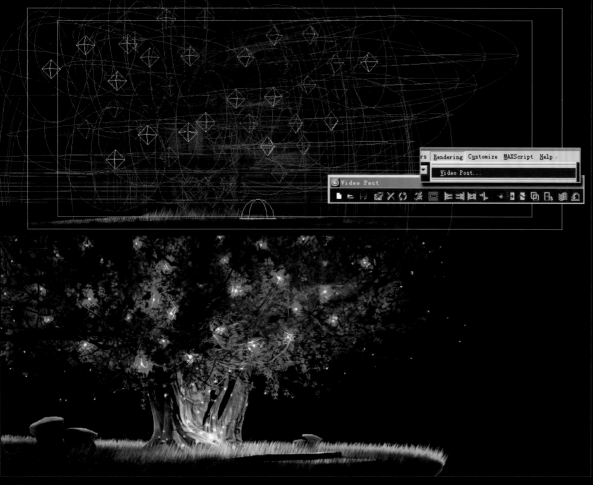

Add lighting effeets

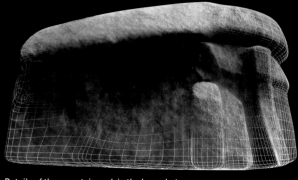

Details of the mountain rock in the long shot,

Create perspective effects by building layers as shown in this illustration.

The designer can enhance the special lighting effects to illustrate the rising sparkles by applying "Video Post" and adjusting the lighting area "Omni." This effect can also be achieved by using the post-production softwares. The entire illustration is themed on a happy atmosphere, as demonstrated by the fiery red tree lit up by the glittering spots.

When working on the elements in the background, the designer should not use too many details to avoid stealing thunder from the major objects. Take the stone in the illustration above for example. A rough outline is enough. The simple is the better.

Similar to the 2D outdoor scene illustrations, the 3D category mainly consists of four parts: the first part is the foreground, the

second is the medium-shot view; the third is given to the atmosphere effect, while the fourth part is the distant view. When working on the entire scene, there is no need to stick to the proportional relationship in a strict way. By keeping perspective principles (the objects at a closer distace from the viewer will look larger) in mind, the designer will succeed in capturing the sense of vastness.

As shown in the left illustration, there is not a huge distance between the viewpoint and the distant mountains. However, due to its tiny size, the mountain will exhibit an optimal perspective effect when we switch to the camera view.

At last, we have to add some elements to enhance the atmosphere, such as the red ribbons flowing between branches and the trajectory of a falling star, to highlight the festive hilarity. "Tree of Happiness" is therefore finished.

The final effect

Add the details and special elements to enhance the atmosphere

Summary

"Atmosphere" is concerned with presenting to the audience scenes and sentiments which can trigger strong responses. Therefore, the intensity of the atmosphere in a certain scene will determine how the audience responds.

Let's use percentages to roughly explain the qualitative changes brought by atmosphere elements: a scene illustration without any atmosphere effect is merely a scenery painting without creativity and inspiration no matter how realistic and exquisite. A scene illustration with 30% atmosphere elements exudes a familiarity with the reality, showing to the audience the beauty of nature. A scene illustration with 60% atmosphere elements has a dramatic touch, inducing the audience to look deeper beyond the illustration. A scene illustration with 90% atmosphere elements is surrealistic in addressing a certain emotional experience. A designer can construct an optimal atmosphere to elevate his illustration to a higher level based on the theme, concept and style.

Gallery

Night

Software: Photoshop

A designer can adjust the illustrating style in order to create some special atmospheres. This illustration has taken advantage of the unique properties of silhouette to highlight a sense of hierarchy. Coupled with lighting effects and color changes, the designer has successfully depicted a serene night in a metropolis.

Sail

Software: Painter

A sail boat is ploughing the roaring waves, with the sky and sea featuring a refreshing blue. There are some fantasy elements with the sail, adding to the romantic atmosphere in the illustration.

Racing

Software: Painter

The designer has made much effort to give prominence to ferocity of the racing car, creating an intense atmosphere.

E. Still Props in Scene Design

Overview

Galery

Overview

Still life in scene design is defined in the same way as in traditional painting, referring to things that cannot move by themselves, including both natural objects and man-made products. The former category includes flowers, plants, seashells, stones and so on, while the latter category encompasses vases, cups, books, jewelry, coins, etc. Still life is an independent discipline in traditional painting. It is an elementary curriculum for beginners and also a necessary training for those who want to perfect their sketching techniques. Many artists have incorporated their personal feelings into their works while striving to make their drawings true to life, giving voices to their emotions through their drawings. In the domain of CG arts, still life is not yet an independent category. In some cases, still life constitutes an integral part of scene illustrations (especially environment illustrations), which can help to highlight the theme, enhance the atmosphere and present the details. Still life is indeed an indispensable constituent for environment illustrations, while on the other hand, scenery is of high importance to still life works. It may be said that some still life works are miniature scene illustrations with a more focused and evident theme. Due to the intimate relationship between scene illustrations and still life works, we have to give an independent chapter to talk about still life, sharing with the readers my experience in this creative profession in the hope that it may offer some inspirations.

I. Fantasy-style and CG Still Life Illustrations

Unlike traditional painting, still life is not categorized as a separate discipline in the domain of CG arts, which explains why it has always fallen victim to neglect. The still life in CG arts often involves unreal objects, some of which are imbued with fantasy elements. Most still life works are used for product exhibition which is function-oriented, while other still frame works have been more and more accepted as gallery collections.

In *Painted Egg*, a blue egg adorned with golden accessories is palmed up by two golden feathers, suspending in the air. The dominant object in the illustration does not look like anything in the real world considering what it looks like and how it is suspended in the air, making the illustration one of the fantasy category. Though there is nothing special about the lighting source and texture, the fantasy elements in the illustration have transformed it from an ordinary still life work into a scene illustration with dramatic effects.

Blue Bee and *Painted Egg* share considerable similarities in terms of color and style. However, the former looks less dramatic than the latter. *Blue Bee* presents a picture which does not differ much from what can be found in real life, if we take no account of the realistic approach, design concept and striking color. It cannot trigger much imagination on the part of audience, which determines that it not as attractive as the other one.

Still life illustrations featuring fantasy style prioritize what the still life objects look like and how they are arranged to enhance the atmosphere and highlight the theme, while its realistic-style counterpart tends to emphasize how to use the best perspective for an optimal visual effect in a limited space, weighing pragmatism over artistic appeal.

Painted Egg — still life illustration

Blue Bee — for product exhibition

Take this illustration for example. The illustration depicts the interior of a store, featuring a reasonable composition, lighting effect and color palette. However, without the existence of still life objects, the picture looks desolate and bleak.

The originally spacious scene has become diversified after the items are added, incorporating more details and changing the theme. The otherwise bleak atmosphere has become boisterous.

II. Concept Development

CG arts are based on computer techniques, which means that CG artists can make full use of its storage of plentiful referential information, diversified drawing tools, and powerful functions. Therefore, artists can unleash their imagination and move beyond the limitations of the real world. 3D softwares can enable the designers to produce amazingly true-to-life works. In 3D still life works, innovative concept, intense atmosphere and rich content are top concerns in the creative process.

In scene illustrations, a designer is supposed to choose suitable still life objects based on the given environment and atmosphere, using them as auxiliary elements to capture the theme. However, in still life works, the still life objects themselves are the highlight of the illustration, which means the designer's choice of what objects to showcase becomes much more important.

Different still life objects will generate different emotional responses, which directly determine what message the illustration delivers to the audience. For example, plants are associated with vitality, while utensils will remind people of their daily life. Concept development is concerned with choosing the right objects, and adding the corresponding dominant color and lighting effect.

Introducing some still life objects that feature unique characteristics to the illustration can give prominence to the style, theme and atmosphere of the work.

III. Basic Composition and Varions Styles

Still life works can be divided into three categories based on the background environment.

The first category uses environment illustrations as background, such as the *Tranquility* on the right. This category shares considerable similarities with environment illustrations. The only difference is that the highlight is the still life object which is placed in a prominent position in the illustration. The object fuses in a perfect way with the background, creating an integral wholeness and an evident sense of gradation, which makes it easier to illustrate the atmosphere and express certain emotions.

The second category is defined by the utilization of a long depth of filed in the background to emulate the "macro shot" effect, like *Chopsticks* in the lower right corner. This category tends to be more attractive to the audience. Due to the long depth of field, the background is easier to produce. The viewpoint is brought closer to the audience, which is a better choice for still life works with complicated structure and meticulous craftsmanship.

The last category includes all the still life works without any concrete background. The *Cacti* in the upper right corner is representative of this category. In this illustration, the background is an abstract space made up of certain color lumps and textures; the highlight is the dominant object, with no concrete background. The designer has projected all his emotions into the depiction of still life objects.

Cacti — still life work without concrete background

Chopsticks — still life work
emulating the macro shot effects

Tranquility — still life work with environment illustration as background

V. Use 3D Softwares to Reproduce Texture

In still life illustrations, the highlight is nothing but the dominant object. Therefore, a designer has to ensure the precision of texture and meticulous depiction, which is a minimum requirement for such illustrations. We can make some preparatory work through observation, such as being sensitive to the texture, glossiness, remaining stains and damage of its surface, and try to capture these characteristics on the corresponding object in illustration to make it true to life.

With the development of 3D software, rendering, lighting and texture effects resemble what is seen in real life. Some 3D still life

works have made more active presence in the CG domain. Designers have become less and less concerned with the pragmatic meaning of their illustrations, but attached more and more importance to their artistic appeal. However, such 3D illustrations still differ from the still life works in traditional painting. The latter mostly involves sketching practice, in which the artist will try to reproduce what a certain object looks like with his drawing pen. How real the illustration looks solely depends on the artist's own experience and techniques. However, the designer has to depend on 3D software in the domain of CG arts. Through complicated calculations, the software will present to the designer precise and veritable light and shade as well as texture effects. By adjusting the position and intensity of the lighting source

and the parameters of the texture mapping, the designer can change the effects of the finish at will in the virtual world. For example, it is easy to come up with a lamplight effect or daylight effect through adjusting the lighting effect, and create metal or glass textures by manipulating the texture.

Though the designer can depend on the powerful functions of 3D softwares to produce true-to-life effects, some meticulous details still need further adjustments. In most cases, it is just these details that determine the artistic values of the illustration.

Capture various textures

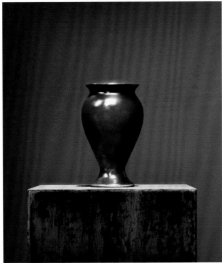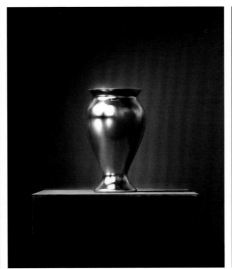

Emulated lighting effect and texture in 3D softwares. From the left to right: daylight effect, lamplight effect, metal texture, and glass texture

"Soaring Together"

V. Case Studies

In the former section for "urban architecture," we have talked about some basic knowledge concerning 3D model construction, texture application and light rendering. In the section on "atmosphere," we have exemplified how to enhance certain atmosphere in 3D scenes through concrete examples. We will go further to explain some 3D drawing techniques, focusing on how to illustrate details in 3D illustrations in this section.

It should be made clear in the first place that we are not intended to encourage the readers to use 3D software by spending so much effort on introducing how to produce 3D illustrations. Instead, we hoped to enable the designers to access more platform tools by exhibiting how various software is employed. Both 2D and 3D illustrations share the same composition framework and theme illustration approach. Therefore, not only 2D artists but also 3D artists will find this section helpful.

a. *Soaring Together*

Soaring Together is inspired by an outdated wooden toy, originally intended to commemorate the happy days of our childhood.

❶ Concept Development

In my childhood, toys were mostly wooden or metal, featuring simple structure and loud colors. They cannot hold a candle to their contemporary counterparts in terms of diversity and entertainment effect. Therefore, we used to invent some special ways to play with these toys, like chasing each other while trying to swing the puppet on others' back. As time goes by, the paint on the puppet has fallen off and childhood companions have set oft for their own dreams. There's always a sense of restraint and vulnerability behind happiness, ahich is the exact message this illustration hopes to convey.

❷ Working on Drafts

It happened such a long time ago that it is difficult to find the toys themselves or photos of them. Therefore, I can only depend on the blurry imagery in my memory. This concept does not seem challenging at first glance, considering that the toy features a simple cubic shape, uniform color and no variation, which means that it does not require outstanding techniques. However, it is just because there is nothing complicated that the designer has to spend more efforts in figuring out how to capture the audience's attention.

❸ 3D Modeling and Mapping

How can we attract the audience's attention through this "simple" still life illustration? A designer has to take account of various elements in order to produce a successful still life work. One has to capture its defining features, and trigger emotional responses to the lifeless object, which certainly takes a lot of thinking.

We will first start with model construction and mapping. The "Platform Toy" which is currently popular has given me a lot of inspirations. Such toys involve painting different patterns on the originally blank surfaces. Therefore, all the toys share an identical shape but differ in color and motif. One of the characteristics of this kind of toy is simplicity, which makes it easier for the designer to give full play to his creativity and imagination. Therefore, I have drawn on the features of "Platform Toys" in designing the toy in the illustration.

Construct a model based on the sketch (by using 3DS MAX). In order to go with mappings of various styles, the model itself should be as simple as possible. There is nothing unique about it except the reversed angle on the frame.

Design sketch

Model construction

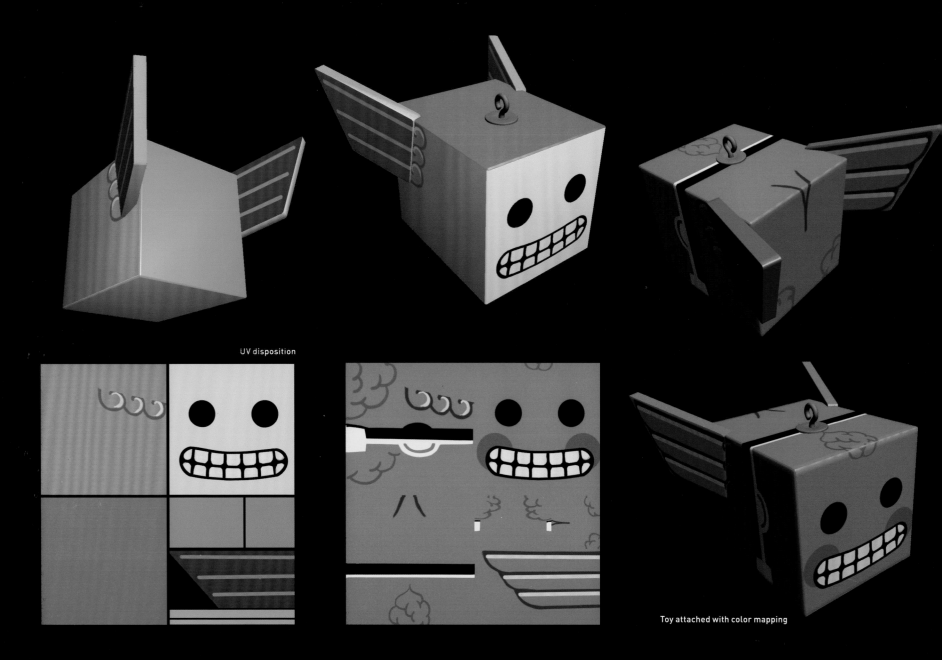

UV disposition

Toy attached with color mapping

According to the design sketch, it can be identified that the angle of view for the final rendering will mainly expose the front and side views of the still life object. Therefore, in addition to the back and the bottom (green areas), other parts will feature a higher UV manipulation. A reasonable application of UV will make it easier for the configurative transfer later.

Draw the first mapping according to the "UV" disposition. Concept for the mapping observes the same rule as the patterns of "Platform Toy" — simple but special. Using large color lumps is a good choice to ensure the integration between different patterns and make it easier to distinguish the unique characteristics of each toy.

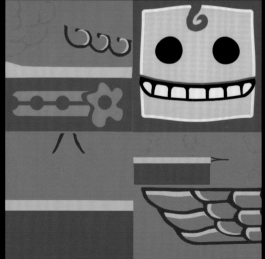
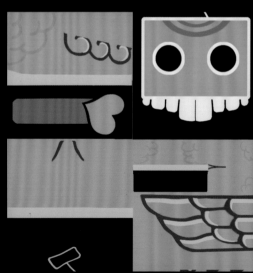
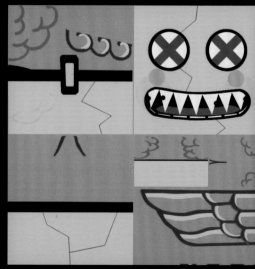

Apply the color mapping to other toys

Finish all the basic mapping for the other characters
following the same approach.

Apply mapping material which emulates
a piece of wood with damaged paint

Put the finished material mapping
to basic color mapping

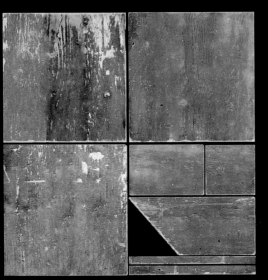

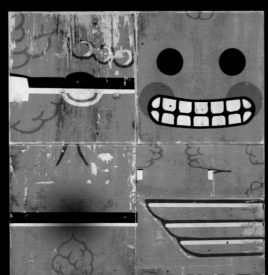

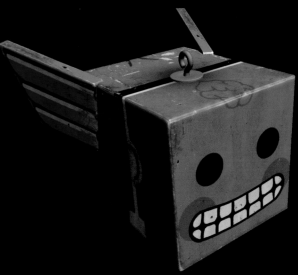

Apply material mapping which emulates a piece of wood with damaged paint. The paint of a timeworn wooden product will fall off due to wear and tear. The bruised part mainly concentrates around the corners and edges. Superimpose the wood texture according to the UV disposition. Deep Paint 3D or Body Paint 3D can be used here to locate the position and integration between the damaged parts in a precise way.

Superimpose the finished wooden texture mapping with the color mapping of the toy to create a finish featuring a nostalgic touch and unique characteristics. The mapping features both bright color and bruised parts. The mapping for scratched wood can be used as the "Bump map" of the toys. The modeling and configuration (mapping) process has come to a conclusion.

The dominant object in the finish

Select the background and decide on the color palette

❹ Elaborating on the Atmosphere

Model and texture constitute the basic elements for a 3D still life illustration. The key is how to infuse vitality into such illustrations. A designer is supposed to depend both elaborating on the details of the dominant object and creating an appropriate atmosphere (it is the same with scene illustrations and still life illustrations). Emulate the wide-angle effect of the fisheye camera to arrange the toys. The first toy is intended as the dominant object, while others serve as a foil. Strike a harmony by matching color and configurations until the illustration is finally finished.

Considering the semi-overlooking view of the model, we choose a bird's-eye-view photo of a lobby as the background. Use the blurring function in Photoshop to emulate the depth of field. As the dominant toy is cherry red, we have chosen a slightly blue color for the background to facilitate a better contrasting and matching effect. Based on the background photo, set up a side lighting source and use "Mental Ray" to render the lighting effect.

Enhance the motion blur and depth of field

Finally, render the model by layers. Set up the depth of vision based on the distance to enhance the sense of gradation. Apply motion blur in areas out of focus to enhance the dynamics of the entire illustration. Add glow at the lighting source and enhance the exposure degree to make the illustration more vivid.

Soaring Together is therefore finished. It features a simple structure, bright color and rich content, which has proved that a seemingly simple still life illustration is also likely to be attractive. By ensuring a vivid mapping, meticulous application of color and harmonized atmosphere rendering, a designer can make interesting and successful work based on a simple dominant object.

b. *The Sofa*

Still life illustrations can be used to demonstrate the unique charisma of a certain still life object and illustrate a certain theme, as shown in the former example. Besides, this category is also a good choice to tell certain stories b=ased on the harmonization of background environment, atmosphere effect and the object itself.

❶ Concept Development

In this still life illustration which uses an interior scene as background, a classical sofa is the highlight of the entire picture. Sunshine finds its way into this gloomy and messy attic, flowing dirt, candlestick and ancient books at side, all indicating that the attic has long been abandoned. The whole illustration is imbued with a classical and obsolete touch. The audience tends to imagine that its owner used to sit on the sofa and look through these books at the candlelight, and lament the desolation with his departure.

❷ 3D Modeling and Mapping

It is advised to first start with the dominant object "sofa." The initial model can be roughly-made. Applying some simple color mapping is enough, because further adjustments will be made in the later process when scene and other objects are added to the illustration. A high-precision model at this stage takes a long time to produce, render and revise in the latter process.

"The Sofa"

Construct a simple model and finish the mapping

❸ The Relationship between the Environment and the Still Life Dominant Object

It is advised to construct the backgrourd attic base on the finished model of the sofa, and then make minor adjustments to the relative position between sofa model and scene model as well as the overall composition. It should be noted that though the environment is gloomy in the original plan, the sofa as the dominant object should be striking. We have drawn inspirations from the classical still life oil paintings by adding lighting sources to the sofa to make it stand out, which will enhance the classical touch and agree with the original concept.

❹ Elaborating on the Details

As this illustration is given to still life, the depth of field effect has been added to the background to create different layers, giving prominence to the dominant object. All the details will disappear when the background is blurred. Therefore, there is no need to spend too much effort on the background; ensuring a consistent style and an intense atmosphere is already enough. When the positions and proportions for all the elements have been determined, we can start to add details to the still life object. I have chosen Zbrush software to depict the details of the model. The details of the material texture should also be enhanced accordingly.

Construct the background attic; adjust the light rendering and composition

Attic with mapping after being rendered

❺ Add Auxiliary Objects, Deal with the Depth of Field and Other Atmosphere Elements

I have added the candlestick and ancient books following my original concept. I had planned to place a table with a matching height to the sofa here to hold these objects. However, I finally gave up this idea in fear that this table would steal thunder from the sofa. Therefore, I have made the candlestick stand on the floor, and a pile of books near the sofa. All these three objects are well connected, forming up a composition featuring a proper density. The floor and distant end of the attic are too spacious; However, by placing some furniture, it would contend with the dominant object for attention. Therefore, I have piled up some unused wood, and make them unrecognizable through the blurring function, diversifying the background without jeopardizing the prominence of the dominant object. At last, atmosphere elements are added, including dirt dancing in the air and the light beams (volume light) admitted from the window. The still life illustration *Sofa* is thus finished.

It is easy to understand the close relationship between the still life works and scene illustrations through *Sofa*. Without the background environment to serve as foil, the still life object will lose its attractiveness, and fails to be that emotionally provocative. On the other hand, by adjusting the composition in the scene and incorporating more props, this still life illustration will become a scene illustration of the interior, which means that sofa will be reduced to an auxiliary element in the scene illustration. Therefore, it is evident how still life works and scene illustrations are interrelated and interdependent.

Elaborate on the dominant object, the sofa.

Enhance the effect and the work is finished.

Summary

Still life illustrations and scene illustrations share considerable similarities. Both categories are concerned with lifeless objects. They celebrate harmony between different objects and attatch importance to the atmosphere. An outstanding still life illustration should exploit the imbedded emotional messages to a full extent. It is the same with scene illustrations. Practice on still life illustrations will help to improve the designer's competence to depict the details, and give better performances when drawing scene illustrations.

Gallery

Offerings for the Temple

Software: 3DS Max

The still life objects in the near shot are positioned in a traditional way. Combined with the scene of the temple in the back, this illustration gives highlights to the details in the front.

Dust

Software: 3DS MAX

Dust obscuring the wine bottle indicates lost time.

The Copper Frog

Software: 3DS MAX

As this work is created a long time ago, the rerdering effect of the software was as perfect as it does today. Digital artists can now produce much more expressive works with the help of advancing softwares. This example may prove that, in this art industry, artist's performance could be restrained due to defects in the softwaves.

Acknowledgements

I want to extend my sincere thanks to Yvonne Zhao, Juan Liu, Sparth, Mingjuan Zhong as well as my friends and families for their supports and assistance in the making of this book. I would also like to thank all the other persons who have helped to edit, design and translate this book. Many thanks to all of you!

Impeccable Scene Design: Scene Design Course by Weiye Yin

Author: Weiye Yin

Project Editor: Yvonne Zhao

English Editor: Dora Ding, Fiona Wong

Translator: Coral Yee

Copy Editor: Lee Perkins

Book Designer: Shiwen Wang, Hong Qiu, Tao Peng

Impeccable Scene Design

© 2011 by China Youth Press, Roaring Lion Media Ltd. and CYP

International Ltd. China Youth Press, Roaring Lion Media Ltd. and CYP

International Ltd. have all rights which have been granted to CYP International

Ltd. to publish and distribute the English edition globally.

First published in the United Kingdom in March 2011 by CYPI PRESS

Add: 79 College Road, Harrow Middlesex, HA1 1BD, UK

Tel: +44 (0) 20 3178 7279

Fax: +44 (0) 19 2345 0465

E-mail: sales@cypi.net editor@cypi.net

Website: www.cypi.co.uk

ISBN: 978-0-9562880-8-0

Printed in China